MW01129825

MERCEDES - BENZ

The Mercedes SLK R170

From the SLK200 to the SLK32 AMG

(1996 – 2004)

By Bernd S. Koehling

Editor: Bevan J. Walsh

First published in December 2014
Second Edition published in October 2015
Third Edition published in February 2017

More information regarding books written by Bernd S. Koehling can be found either at the end of this book or here:
www.benz-books.com

ISBN-10: 1505421500
ISBN-13: 978-1505421507

Printed in the United States

KOMPRESSOR

CONTENT

Technical chapters

FOREWORD

First of all I would like to thank you for having purchased this book. I hope you will enjoy reading it as much as I enjoyed writing it. This book covers the SLK R170, built from 1996 until 2004 with all its variations, AMG version, special editions and some of the tuner activities with vehicles from Brabus, Väth Carlsson and RENNtech. Although there were a lot more companies around that dealt in one way or another with tuning the small roadster, it would have been impossible to cover them all, so I ask for your forgiveness, that the list that made it into this book is not exhaustive.

When the R170 was first shown in 1994 at the Turin auto show as a concept car, it was a surprise to everyone, who was a bit familiar with Daimler-Benz. Although a German car magazine was already speculating in 1990 that something was "cooking", nobody had expected a small sports car the size of the Mazda Miata. For Daimler-Benz it was not just a new car in a new segment, it was a quantum leap forward. The SLK put the company at once ahead of its archrivals Porsche and BMW, which had or were to introduce similarly sized cars. When one saw it in its final version in 1996 with its fully automatic vario-roof, one had to admit that it was not just a clever marketing approach, but a technical master piece that should prove over the years surprisingly reliable. The folding metal top was indeed so popular that other manufacturers would, over the next couple of years, install them in numerous other convertibles. The idea even made it into the iconic Mercedes-Benz SL, debuting in R230 form in 2001.

From the beginning, the SLK R170 was a big hit with roadster aficionados. It was offered in colors and interior variations that would have been previously unthinkable in a Mercedes. And it was aimed at a clientele that would have never considered a Mercedes as their car of first choice. For them it did not seem to matter that its smallest engine initially produced just 136 hp. The car was hip and everybody wanted one. So it was no wonder that Daimler-Benz had in the first year huge problems coping with unexpected demand.

After the success of the 190SL (W201), the SLK was only the second entry into a market segment that Daimler-Benz had left untouched since the 1930s. And as history has shown, it was not the last such offering.

I would like to thank Daimler AG for the support I received from the extremely helpful staff at the company's archive. Special thanks have also to go to slkworld.com and benzworld.org for the invaluable information I was able to gather from their input. This is the third edition of the 2014 book. It contains the latest used car prices from early February 2017, more recent photos have been added and its technical information is more detailed.

February 2017
Bernd S. Koehling

Mercedes-Benz SLK R170 series

1996 - 2004

How it all began

Whoever wants to know more about the small SL, the SLK, will at some point also seek to understand the vehicle concept`s history. After all, similar names were used by Daimler-Benz way back in the 1920s and 1930s, in cars synonymous with racing success across Europe. The vehicles, to which I am referring, were instrumental in establishing the Mercedes brand as a major factor in the sports car market. Of course, the huge and powerful SS (Super Sport), SSK (Super Sport Kurz) and SSKL (Super Sport Kurz Light) of those days had almost nothing in common with their "tiny" modern cousin.

Still, such a relationship, even though just through similar names, never hurts. In order to find other connections within the long and esteemed Daimler-Benz history, one has to look to the 1950s. A certain Max Hoffman, well known for urging the creation of, and then importing attractive European sports cars into the New World, had pushed the executive board of Daimler-Benz to create a special automobile that would help him sell their cars in North America. This car would be responsible for effectively introducing the Mercedes brand to a larger group of potential customers in the US than the small circle then already familiar with the brand. The car carrying so much responsibility was, of course, the 300SL Gullwing, first shown to the American public at the 1954 New York automobile show

However, even prior to the launch of the iconic SL, Daimler-Benz management were discussing with Hoffman the notion that a smaller, more affordable roadster would be a beneficial addition to such an important market as North America. After they had finally agreed on the design, it took Daimler-Benz stylists just eight weeks to get from blueprints to a first 1:1 scale model. The car was of course the 190SL. And it stood side by side with the 300SL at said show in 1954.

For both, Daimler-Benz and Hoffman, the decision to offer a smaller SL was entirely market driven. Everybody knew that the ultra-expensive 300SL would not sell in large numbers. But everybody also knew that a more affordable, similarly styled roadster would attract a much bigger crowd that was intrigued by the aura of the Über-SL, but not necessarily by the price tag that came with it.

Had it been only for the 300SL, the SL sports car would not have seen a successor. After all, counting coupe and roadster sales together, a mere 3,258 units sold (coupe: 1,400, roadster: 1,858) between 1954 to 1963. That means on average less than 30 cars a month found homes. Compare this to the "lesser" SL, of which a respectable 25,881 units sold between 1955 and 1963, which convinced the executive board to go ahead with the development of a new version of the SL. As we all know, that was the 230SL launched in 1963, commonly known as the Pagoda.

A 1929 Model SSK

The prototype 190SL in 1954 in New York

Fast forward to 1989:

After the long and successful career of Pagoda successor, the R107, the R129 was launched in 1989. Initial production was planned for 20,000 units annually. Although prices for the new roadster reached almost stratospheric levels, demand far outweighed supply. At the top end of the convertible car market, the SL had no rivals in its price range. Capacity at the newly opened Bremen plant was soon increased to 25,000 units annually, but to no avail: the waiting list hovered at around two years and could even reach up to five years for rare models in unique color and equipment options. The situation was similar to that in the 1970s, when there was a famous saying among German farmers who had ordered a Mercedes Diesel sedan: "I can cope with draughts and floods, but not with the long waiting list for my new diesel".

And then in 1990 suddenly everything changed: the Mazda MX5 Miata hit earth. Although it was not really a threat to the upper end of the convertible car market, Daimler-Benz management knew instantly: this was a game changer. Of course, there were other convertibles available at that time. The Cadillac Allante, produced from 1987 to 1993, was an attempt by GM to steal some of the SL's glamour. Although it was a bargain compared with the SL and although it offered the state-of-the-art Northstar DOHC V8, people did not warm to it in sufficient numbers.

Mazda Miata (MX5) from 1991 and Cadillac Allante (next page) from 1992

In addition, flying it during its production process from Italy (Pininfarina had designed it and built the body) to the US in an exclusive deal with Lufthansa Cargo did not exactly help the bottom line. So when sales failed to impress management, the project was abandoned. Overall, just 21,430 Allantes were built. Cadillac tried the convertible market again only in 2003 with the XLR. But this time, with a retractable metal hardtop designed and built by a joint venture company of Mercedes and Porsche, which also supplied the SLK's vario-roof.

The lovely Ford Mustang (especially with its 5.0L engine) was a joy to drive, but was not offered by Ford outside the US. Much cheaper than the SL, it was also not meant to be a match for the SL's build quality. And the BMW Z1 with its troublesome disappearing doors (and lots of interesting technical features for its time) was offered as a limited edition model with just 8,000 units sold from 1989 to mid-1991.

The Miata was different. It made people suddenly realize that open-top driving was within their financial reach. The small car was not only attractively priced and soundly engineered: on top of that, it was gorgeous to look at and managed to hit the emotional soft spot in most drivers, both male and female. As a consequence of all of this, it was THE car to be seen in. This included "the rich and famous". Their today's Prius was the Miata in the early 1990s. What the British had achieved so successfully in the years after WWII with cars such as the brilliant MG TC and later the MG A/MG B, the Japanese had now simply copied.

And it is somewhat ironic that a team from Mazda had spent quite some time on the stand of the British "Stevens Cipher" roadster at the 1980 Birmingham Motor Show in the UK. Their later mission statement for the Miata is supposed to be a straight copy of the press release for the Cipher (according to Prof. Tony Stevens, Chairman of Stevens Research Ltd).

Daimler-Benz (together with other car companies) was keenly aware that this "small convertible niche" would not just grow at the rate of the overall automotive market - no, they realized that it would grow by leaps and bounds. And this would happen not only in the US and in Europe, but all over the world. They urgently needed some presence in this niche. Not at the price level of the Mazda. That was not their domain (yet), but size-wise their new Mercedes-Benz convertible had to be much smaller (and more affordable) than the R129.

It was rather fitting that the company had launched, after an absence of some fifty years, a mid-prized sedan in form of the 190 W201 in 1982. A small and affordable roadster would make a more than welcome addition to this new line of cars and it was only natural that there was some parts-sharing from the new W202 C-class with the R170 sports car. After all, it was the same practice as Daimler-Benz had employed in the 1950s with the 180/190 sedan and the 190SL.

The new baby-SL could not just be a slightly larger Miata on steroids, which Daimler-Benz could sell at a premium. They knew the new car had to come with a twist, a USP that nobody would have expected from this tradition-minded company. Luckily, the days were long gone, when Daimler-Benz was regarded by journalists as an automotive manufacturer that would only produce high quality cars for executives, farmers and well-healed retirees.

The concept cars

The German automotive magazine *auto motor und sport* reported as early as 1990 that Daimler-Benz was to introduce a small SL and envisioned that its launch was to occur in 1992. As we all know, that did not transpire. The first of two studies was shown to the public in April 1994 at the Turin auto show. It was not the most prestigious location for a concept car that should take the automotive world by storm. But Italy had always been associated with unique cars and advanced designs and maybe also the fact that head of Daimler-Benz design, Bruno Sacco, was Italian itself contributed to the selection of this venue for the car´s first public appearance.

Almost at the same time, the car was shown on German TV, when head of engineering Dieter Zetsche presented it on a Late Night Show, hosted by German entertainer Thomas Gottschalk. This was a first for Daimler-Benz, who normally choose the Geneva auto show to debut their new sports car stars. Management must have felt that a car that was born into the dotcom era, for a clientele that was markedly younger than the average Mercedes owner, necessitated a new vibe for its presentation. Hence the young Dieter Zetsche, who did not appear on TV in his usually dark suit, but showed up in jeans and a green sports jacket.

The car was a stunner. Equipped with a fabric top (not shown on any of the car's official photos, so was it really there?) it offered rollover bars with rear covers resembling those of the famous 300SLR from the 1950s. The small sports car used a four-cylinder, four-valve engine, mated to a five-speed manual on a custom-designed platform. Both front and rear axles were borrowed from the C-class, and had it been registered, it would have been fully drivable on public roads. With its brilliant-silver paint scheme, it oozed a distinct aura of frugal sportiness in a compact design.

Bruno Sacco had made clear, what he expected the car to be. It should track as much as possible the aesthetic qualities of the larger SL R129 by showing vertical affinity and horizontal homogeneity with that car.

During final development, the front fenders with a slight 190SL theme were redesigned

The first concept cars had a rather colorful interior

It should offer a unique synthesis of motoring pleasure with all the safety features for which Mercedes cars were renowned for. On top of all this, Sacco said it needed to address the emotional side of driving. It should help to give its proud owner a feeling of freedom, independence and even adventure. Naturally, it carried the genes of most sports car designs: a long hood, low windscreen, wide doors and a short, muscular looking rear. But Sacco also stressed that it should not portray a form that just followed current automotive styling trends. That would not be Mercedes design language.

From over twelve 1:5 gypsum models, five made it to 1:1 scale versions. Finally in 1993 the executive board gave the green light to a design proposal by Michael Mauer, who was from 1992 to 1995 head of interior and exterior design for the A-class, the SL - and the SLK. He started with Daimler-Benz in 1986 in Sindelfingen and after the SLK success, from 1998 to 1999 headed the Advanced Design office in Japan, before he became head of design for the Daimler-Benz subsidiary Smart. In 2000, he joined Saab to become their head of design. With the subsequent decline of Saab, though, he saw no real future for himself in GM, so in 2004 he landed a dream job: he was asked to succeed Harm Lagaay at Porsche, who retired after 15 years as head of design there. Porsches that can be fully attributed to Mauer are the Panamera, the second-generation Cayenne, and the super car 918 Spyder.

Michael Mauer

A design patent was filed at the Munich based German patent office in September 1993. Within 16 weeks of hard and diligent work and after having spent DM 3 million (US $1.9 million at a 1993 exchange rate), the first concept car was ready to be presented to the eager automotive world. Keeping an eye on the larger SL, the car carried the name SLK for *Short, Light* and *Compact.* Its front, the short overhangs and a pronounced wedge shape all hinted at its affinity with the larger and more expensive brother. It was, as the official Daimler-Benz language suggested, an unconventional, future-oriented interpretation of the SL-theme. The traditional SL front felt somewhat rejuvenated with headlights that resembled the ones of the big S-class coupe C140. Other hints at the SL tradition were the two power-domes in the hood, which should draw a line to the 300SL (the 190SL only had one). It's wheelbase of 2,400 mm (94.5 in) was identical with that of the 190SL (and 300SL as a matter of fact). But with its short overhangs, making for an overall length of 3,995 mm, it was somewhat shorter (versus the 4,220 mm length of the 190SL). The final SLK was, with its safety features and vario-roof, some 15 percent heavier than its spiritual predecessor. A curb weight of 1,365 kg for the SLK200 compared with 1,180kg for the 190SL including hardtop.

The 300SLR-type roll-over bar covers were unique to the first concept car

The interior impressed with gleaming metal surfaces. Only twenty percent of it was covered with red leather. Another design element was a lightweight carbon-fiber dashboard, which should give an airy, even floating feeling inside the car. Its front was again covered with red leather. Two stowage nets underneath supported the minimalistic interior approach. The instruments and ignition lock were each surrounded by an aluminum rim, as was the short gearshift lever on the center console. In order to continue with the approach to an impression of lightness and minimalism, the three pedals for clutch, brake and accelerator were made of perforated aluminum. The gearshift lever and steering wheel were covered with carbon fiber, and the seats with red and silver-grey leather.

Six months later the second concept car was presented at the Paris auto show. This time it had taken the design team twelve weeks and an additional DM 2 million (US $1.27 million). Also this car was fully drivable. But now the car´s interior theme was not lightness, this time (we are in Paris after all), it was elegance, opulence, and much fine orange leather.

There was no more gleaming metal: everything including the floor was covered with leather or blue alcantara.

As blue was the traditional French racing color, the concept car was painted blue. Specification included automatic transmission, air-conditioning, power windows and a hi-fi sound system. With the rollover bars now exposed, the bodywork of this second car differed otherwise only in small details from its Turin sibling. But of course there was one big, significant difference: the vario-roof! Daimler-Benz and Porsche had earlier decided to form a new company to develop and build this new top's mechanism.

At the push of a button, the electro-hydraulic roof transformed the SLK from a convertible to a coupe or vice versa in just 25 seconds. Daimler-Benz was the first company to revive a concept in larger numbers that dated back to the 1930s. It became so popular that numerous other car manufacturers copied the idea. If one wants to know more about the roof`s origin, one has to travel back in time not only to the 1930s, but actually the 1920s. And in case you are interested in the history of the vario-roof, then the next chapter is for you. Otherwise, please proceed to the SLK vario-roof chapter that follows it.

The previous metal surfaces were covered with leather and alcantara

First view of the vario-roof. It should prove surprisingly reliable

History of the vario roof

In most publications the interested reader will discover that the first car equipped with a folding-hardtop roof was a Peugeot 401 from 1934. This is correct, when one considers electrical hardtops only. But this is just half the story, as the concept to have an all-weather removable metal top in an automobile dates back further. And it did not start in France, but in the United States of America. Benjamin Ellerbeck from Salt Lake City, Utah was an engineer with a keen interest in everything automotive. By autumn 1919 he had worked out the basic design of a shiftable/retractable top for open cars, and by the early 1920s he had built a number of 1/8 scale models to demonstrate how his invention worked to potential clients. In 1921, he was granted a patent (US patent no. 1.379.906) for his shiftable top. Jumping forward somewhat, in December 1930 he was granted another US patent for a roadster that featured a second windshield for the rumble seat.

Although he was fairly enthusiastic about his invention, he had so far failed to attract a major customer to apply his ideas. Therefore, in 1922 Ellerbeck bought a 1919 Hudson Super Six, to serve as real world model for his innovative top. In order to make his new roof fit, he had to rebuild major parts of the Hudson. But the result was an attractive car, which looked especially inviting with the top down. Once closed, the overhang above the windshield looked similar to a giant air scoop or sun visor.

One problem was the fairly complicated mechanism to manually raise and lower the top. Costly to produce, it scared off quite a few possible customers. So in 1923 he changed his creation by letting the roof rest on landau bars, which were secured to the ends of a cross shaft passing through the body. The previous creation offered straight diagonal arms, which were located inside of both body and top. The top was a metal frame with either fabric or metal cover. In lowered position, it would settle flush on the rear deck. In both lowered and raised positions it was secured with clamps.

Still, despite his design changes, he had not found an interested party for the innovative top. So in 1925 he wrote a lengthy letter to Packard Motor Company, trying to interest them in his creation. In his letter he stated that he understood the car manufacturer's desire to draw the line somewhere in the diversity of body styles.

Then he continued in his letter that he was convinced a Packard roadster would leap in favor if given a modern top construction. Unfortunately, Packard declined, but this did not stop his enthusiasm for his design.

Ellerbeck even managed to get his design covered in an article by a British car magazine in the early 1930s, but also saw no interest forthcoming from any foreign manufacturer. The 1929 stock market crash and following economic crisis certainly did not help and when interest in roadsters decreased towards the mid-1930s, so too did all effort from Benjamin Ellerbeck, who had fought so hard for over 15 years to have his innovative concept accepted. Like so many good ideas, it was probably ahead of its time.

The top for the Hudson was altered, as it now sat on top of the car's rear section

An opening in the roof left room for additional passengers

Although almost forgotten, the concept was not dead entirely. A French dentist, who, just like Ellerbeck, held a keen interest in everything automotive, picked up Ellerbeck´s idea in 1930 in Europe. Because next to making a living as a dentist, George Paulin was also a gifted part-time automobile designer. The shiftable top concept was re-evaluated, simplified and it finally evolved under Paulin into the first power-operated retractable hardtop and consequently was patented by him in 1931.

On his side of the Atlantic, no one showed any interest, initially, in his concept either. Luckily, however, in autumn 1933 that changed, when Peugeot`s Paris car dealer Emile Darl`mat (a friend of Paulin), introduced the dentist to French coachbuilder Marcel Pourtout. Pourtout was immediately intrigued by Paulin´s patent and all three worked on making the retractable top happen. It was Paulin's luck to have a large car dealer and a respected coachbuilder at his side, support that Ellerbeck unfortunately never enjoyed.

In May 1934, Carosserie Pourtout used a mid-sized Peugeot 402BL, supplied by Darl`mat, to introduce its Eclipse Decapotable (retractable roof). The revolutionary car gained considerable news coverage, which in turn brought Peugeot management into contact with Paulin. In 1935, he convinced the company of the virtues of his novel concept and consequently sold them his patent.

In order to further support the idea, Paulin worked from 1934 till 1938 as Pourtout`s designer and helped to launch the system on cars such as the Peugeot 301, 401 and 601. 79 of Peugeot Type 401 and 473 of Peugeot Type 402 were produced with this roof. Sufficient space for the large metal roof was vital, so of all vehicles some 400 were built on the extended sedan chassis of the "Familiale Limousine", which had a length of some 5,30 m (210.4 in). The extended chassis made the cars relatively expensive.

To mitigate that, it was decided to offer those cars with a manually operated top only. Most customers did not mind, since it was relatively easy to manually raise or lower the top. Sadly, only 34 Eclipse Decapotables survived today. Other vehicles designed with a retractable roof by Paulin and produced by Pourtout include the Italian Lancia Belna and various models from French car manufacturers Hotchkiss and Panhard.

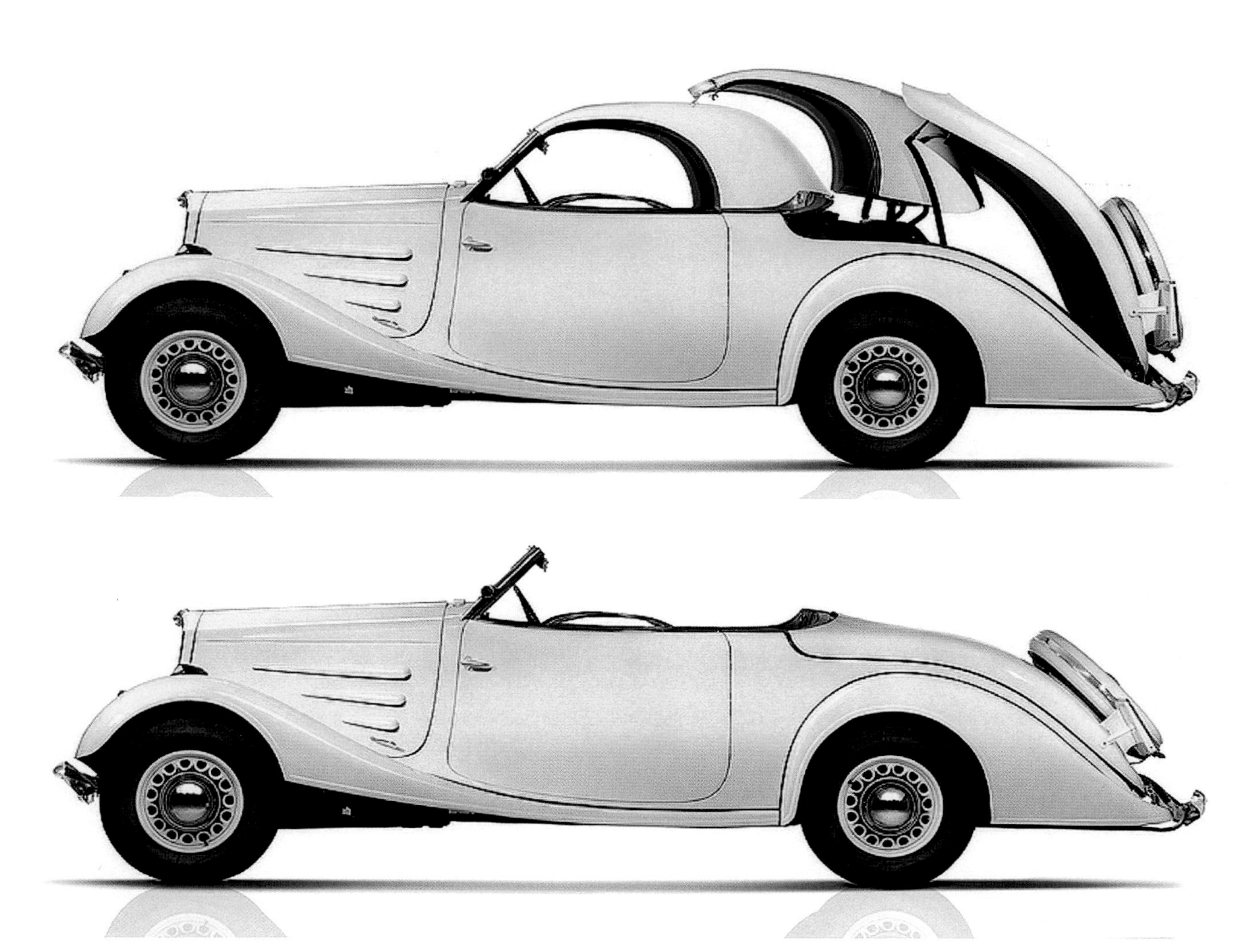

Peugeot 401 Eclipse: once the top was lowered, there was no luggage space left

The first American car to feature a retractable hardtop after the failed Ellerbeck attempt was the 1941 Chrysler Thunderbolt Roadster, produced to help improve Chrysler`s image among consumers. It must have been one of the first American dream cars and was designed by Alex Tremulis. Four of the five Thunderbolt ever built are known to have survived.

Ford picked up the idea of a retractable hardtop in 1956 to offer a Fairlane 500 Skyliner for the model years 1957 to 1959. The Skyliner was a full-sized two-door offer with a fairly complex electrically-operated hardtop. The top had a fold at the front, which disappeared with the rest of the roof under a long trunk lid. Compared with the Peugeot roof, this was a pure high-tech design.

The 1941 Chrysler Thunderbolt Roadster. Very little is known about these cars. Its turning radius must have been huge

Ford Fairlane 500 Skyliner: the roof looked complicated, but was reliable and must have been stunning to watch in motion in the 1950s

The Ford Fairlane driver did not have to do anything but to push a single button, and everything else happened as if by magic. The system was equipped with three electric motors that drove four jacks to lift and stow the top, four locking mechanisms to hold the top in place, ten solenoids and another four electric motors to lock the doors and trunk. Each of the seven electrical motors had its own circuit breaker and 186 m (610 ft) of wiring was required to make this all work. The big Ford was with a length of 5.35 m (210.8 in) just 5 mm longer than its French predecessor, which did not have the split roof. And according to period reviews, the Ford´s top worked reliably, despite its complicated set-up. In those three years of production, Ford sold a total of 38,394 units.

Mitsubishi offered, in 1995 and 1996, a special edition of its 3000GT model. It was shipped from its Nagoya, Japan factory to ASC (American Sunroof Company) in California in coupe form. In California, it was transformed to the first modern car with a folding hardtop, and called "3000GT Spyder". Like the Ford Skyliner, the roof opened fully automatic with the push of a button. With only 1,618 units sold, it was abandoned in 1996. It can be assumed that the car was Mitsubishi's quick answer to the 1994 SLK presentation in Turin and Paris. But shipping it first from Japan to ASC, where the top had to be chopped off, the chassis strengthened and the folding hardtop installed, made it a pretty expensive exercise. Therefore, it was no wonder that sales remained low and the project was quickly abandoned.

The interesting Mitsubishi 3000GT Spyder was unfortunately killed by its high price

The SLK vario roof

Daimler-Benz coined the term vario-roof, to refer to the folding-metal hardtop engineered for their cars. Like Ford, they had problems stowing the hardtop away in one piece, especially as the rear of the car was relatively short. It had to be divided in two halves, which were linked by a kinematic mechanism that was automatically locked when the roof was closed.

At the touch of a button on the center console, a hydraulic system with five cylinders controlled the folding process. This included the opening and closing of the trunk lid, which opened by tipping to the rear. This was necessary, because that way the two roof halves had enough space to pivot backwards. But this process also meant that a minimum clearance height of 1.65 m (5.5 ft) and an additional 0.25 m (10 in) length behind the SLK was required to lower or raise the hardtop. When the roof opened, its two sections positioned themselves one on top of the other just before being stowed inside the trunk. This impressive sequence was naturally reversed when the roof was closed. The roof`s front latch hydraulic cylinders were located under the front edge of the roof and above the top center portion of the windshield frame.

The roof created quite a stir in the early SLK days

Owners had to get used to the tiny opening, once the roof was lowered

The hydraulic system stowed the roof parts in the upper section of the trunk. A plastic roller blind separated it from the luggage space below to prevent luggage items from colliding with the roof components. This luggage cover could be extended (a prerequisite to opening the roof) or retracted in order to maximize luggage space, provided the owner kept the roof closed for the duration. Top down, the trunk offered a capacity of 145 l (5.1 cu ft). This should be sufficient for two not too-large-sports bags. With the top out of the way, the load volume increased to a more respectable 348 l (12.3 cu ft). In this mode, cases with tall water bottles could be stowed. The driver could operate the hardtop only when the car was not exceeding a speed of 8 km/h (5 mph).

Back in 1996, the process of opening or closing the hardtop was fairly impressive for many onlookers. How did it work in real life? The driver only had to hold the hardtop switch in the center console in its forward position. First, the indicator lamp in the switch lighted up, then the door and rear quarter windows lowered and the trunk lid opened rearward.

Next the two-part hardtop came out of its storage compartment, while at the same time the shelf behind the two roll bars opened and the small rear quarter windows closed again. Then the shelf behind the roll bars plus the trunk lid closed again and the hardtop locked securely in place. Finally, the indicator lamp went off and the whole procedure was over. As already mentioned, all of this occurs within 25 seconds. The Ford Skyliner of the 1950s took some sixty seconds for this operation. A remote for the top only became available with the second generation SLK, as an after-market device.

Naturally, the electro-hydraulic Vario roof is the main USP of the SLK, and according to the SLK R170 project manager, Jörg Prigl, required much wizardry from their engineers. Twelve engineers had been in charge of its development and testing. When regularly maintained, it is as reliable today as the rest of the car. If not cared for, though, the hardtop has the nasty habit of turning into the car´s most troublesome feature. The aforementioned five hydraulic cylinders, four window motors, a hydraulic pump, a relay, nine limit switches, a control switch, two solenoids, one control module plus tons of wiring to make it all work in sync, can make even the most elegant mechanical device fail.

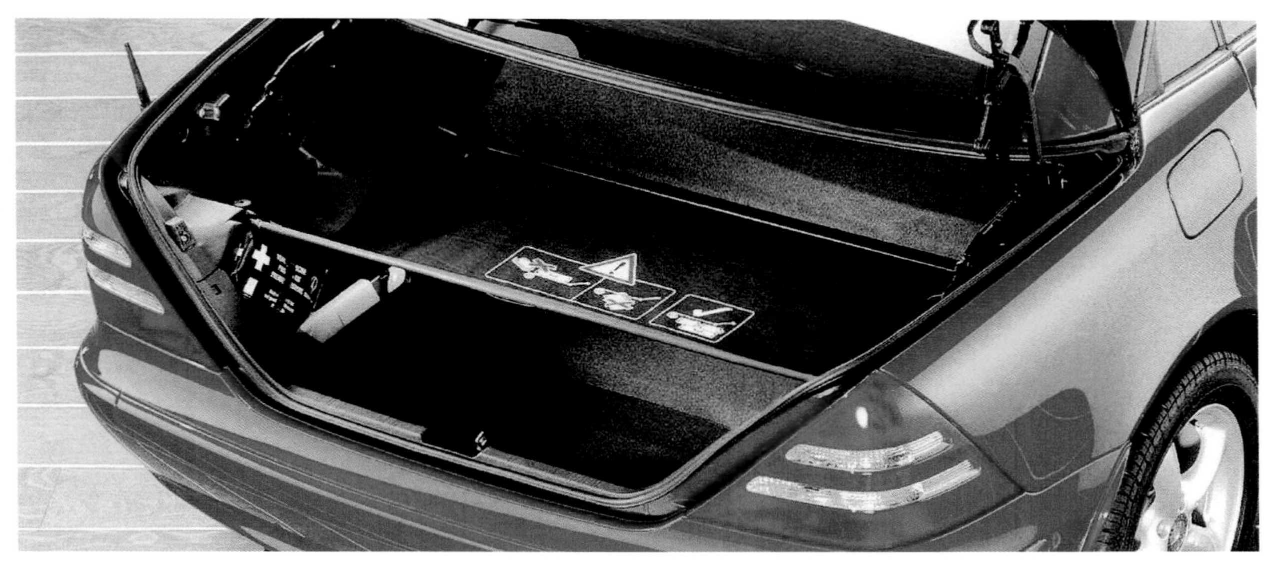

The extendable plastic cover should prevent scratches on the top. Also in order to make the top work, it needed to be in that position

Luggage space was sufficient, when the top was raised

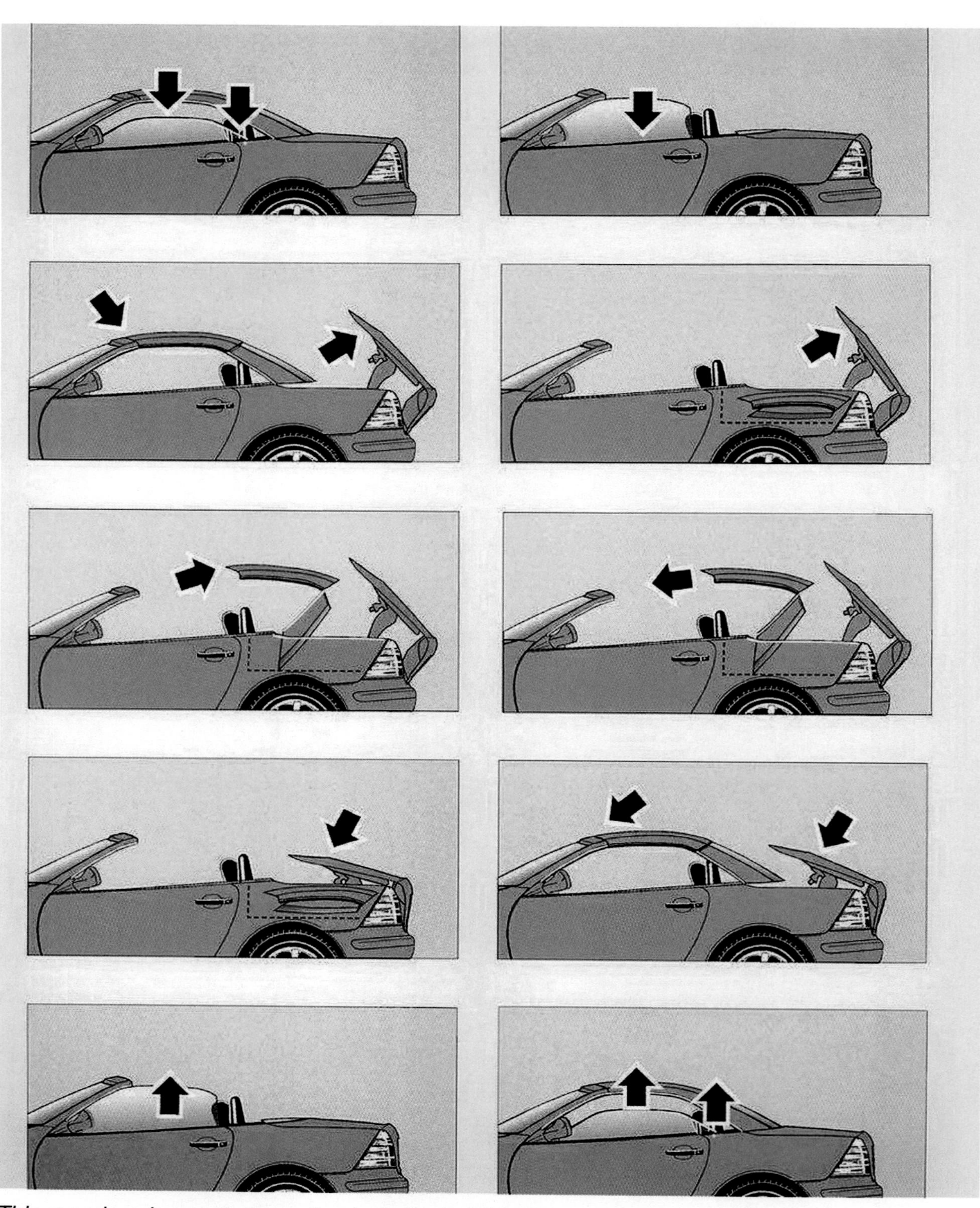

This overview demonstrates quite nicely the individual movements of the vario roof

The standard draft blocker was made out of fabric

There are various after-market options available. But they are not more effective

Trouble-shooting the vario roof

The tips that follow are intended to serve as general guide only, since our primary focus here is the history of the SLK. However, it is hoped that this will be helpful to some readers.

If the top stops functioning, the first and easiest thing to check is the plastic luggage cover in the trunk, which should be closed in the rear position, meaning it should be hooked into the upper rear post holders. We mentioned earlier that the roof can only be opened if the luggage cover is pulled to the rear. Sometimes the contact switch for the luggage cover needs a bit of cleaning to relay the message "yes, I am in position, start working".

A healthy, charged battery should have at least 11.4 volts with the engine switched off. If that is the case and the roof still refuses to cooperate, the hardtop switch on the center console may be at fault. If its internal lamp is blinking slowly, there is a system malfunction that can only be properly diagnosed by a technician. If the internal lamp is not lighting, the connections could have deteriorated over the years. By removing the rear part of the center console, one can access the switch and can check its connections.

If the switch and its connections seem to be in order, the focus should then be on the combination control module under the hood on the passenger's side. As the name implies, the module controls the hydraulic unit (and tells it to change direction of pump motor rotation) and the side window motors. It reads switch position and sensor values and sends function and warning messages. It also controls the wipers, central locking and rear window defroster.

This key part of the system is unfortunately quite expensive (> US$800) to replace. Luckily, it is fairly reliable, and in the event of a problem here, try disconnecting and then reconnecting the module's cable – it may be all that's needed.

The hydraulic pump with its oil reservoir on the right and the black relay in front below the blue-white sign

Another focus should be the relay for the hydraulic pump, which is located at the right side of the trunk, hidden behind the side paneling. When the hardtop switch is pushed, the relay should make a clicking sound. If that does not happen, it needs to be checked with a multi-meter to confirm that power is being sent to it. If no power is measured, either the hardtop switch or the wiring from the switch to the relay could be damaged. If there is power, but one cannot hear any clicking sound, the best thing to do is replace the (not expensive) relay. And even if the relay is clicking, small internal parts could have worn out over the years, so that insufficient power is sent to the hydraulic unit to operate the hardtop. Replacing the relay also, in this circumstance, might solve the problem.

If the operation of the hardtop is slow, cleaning and greasing the hinges can be of help. A regular lubing of all pivot points will improve the top's operation. In addition, the hydraulic pump's fluid level needs to be checked - the level can be viewed through its access door on the pump. The fill hole is on top of the pump. In order to get to it, the metal cover above it needs to be removed first.

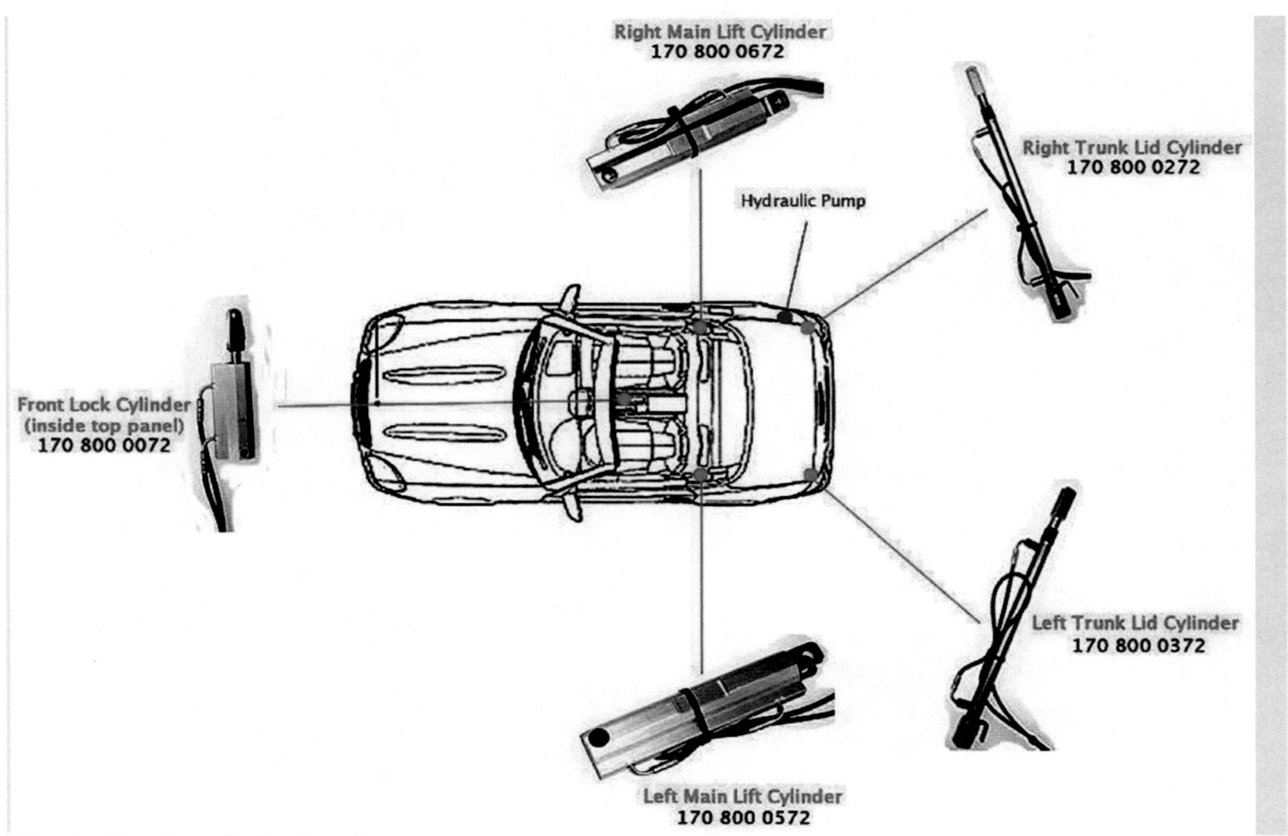

The hydraulic cylinder locations

This rarely happens, but a low fluid level can mean that there is a leak in the system either at the pump itself or at one of the hydraulic cylinders. Four of them are located at each corner of the trunk, the fifth one is installed above the headliner.

Occasionally SLKs have issues with the top stuck halfway up. This could be caused by hardened rubber boots, which cover the sensor switches that let the tops go up and down. Replacing the boots is fairly inexpensive.

Another possible reason for the top not to open or close completely can be a loose/hanging flap under the trunk lid. There are two of them and they are located close to the passenger compartment. Daimler-Benz offers a repair-kit for the flap problem.

The picture on the following page should only serve as rough guideline on how to use the kit and tighten the flaps, because this is a job better left to an experienced mechanic. If one still wants to do it, it is best to ask the vendor for instructions. If one is a novice, be prepared to spend the better part of three to four hours to fix it.

MODEL 230.467 /474 /475 /476 /479

1 *Side flap drive*
2 *Side flaps*
3 *Trunk lid*
4 *Locknut* 17 MM Open End Wrench
5 *Adjusting nut* = 12 MM Open End Wrench

The four Screws that come with the Kit are self-threading

The Repair Kit Part # is 2307500111-22 and it is carried by koperformance.com, parts.con and others

The Adjusting Nut Wrench needs to be thinner that a normal 12 MM Wrench when used to untighten the Lock Nut. Fortunately I had a small Crescent Wrench that worked.

NOTE: To make the flap fit tighter against the trunk lid when it is all the way up turn the adjusting nut clockwise and vice versa to make it looser.

You should also know that in order to install the repair kit pieces you will need, besides the wrenches, a number 10 Torx Driver or Bit and a Number 30 Torx Driver or Bit.

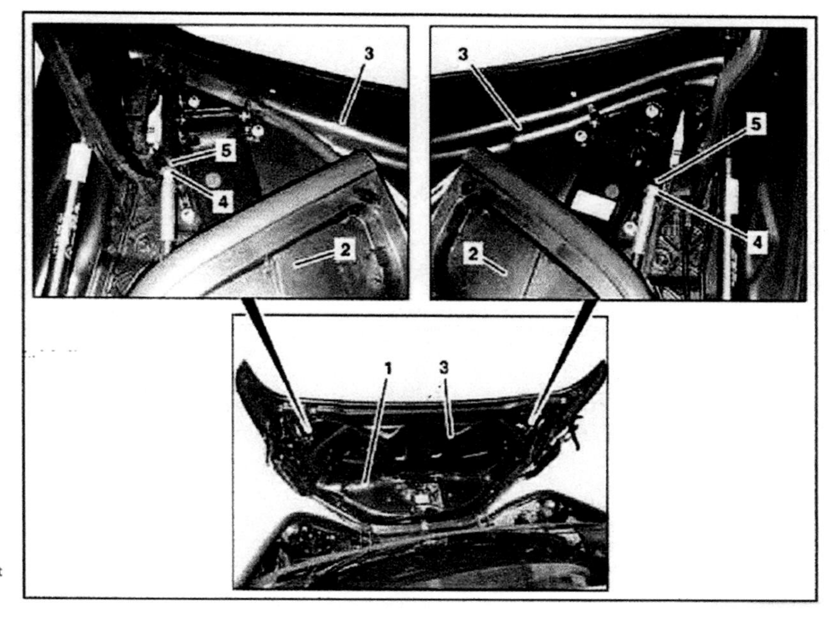

And sometimes when the top refuses to co-operate, it's the good old-fashioned (gentle) shaking the top back and forth that will possibly remedy the situation, while a second person operates the switch. This might help especially, when the top seals might get stuck at the windshield frame. A push on the roof near the windshield frame and proper cleaning and applying talcum powder or rubber grease ("Gummi-Pflege" in German) on the seals can be an easy remedy.

These are just some of the inexpensive ways to fix issues with the hardtop and hopefully for the wallet of the SLK owner, a possible malfunctioning can be associated with one of them. It gets progressively more expensive, when the wiring or hydraulic cylinders are at fault. While switches, relays and cable connections can be replaced fairly inexpensively, a new hydraulic cylinder, if it cannot be repaired, is expensive. And as we already know, there are five of them. Over time their seals decay and if they are allowed to crumble apart, the particles may block the valves in the pumps.

There are numerous websites, which offer all kinds of assistance and are a great source for any information around the SLK (and of course most other Mercedes models). I would like to mention just a few, although there are many others: the most specific to everything SLK is: *http://www.slkworld.com* and that is why it is highly recommended.

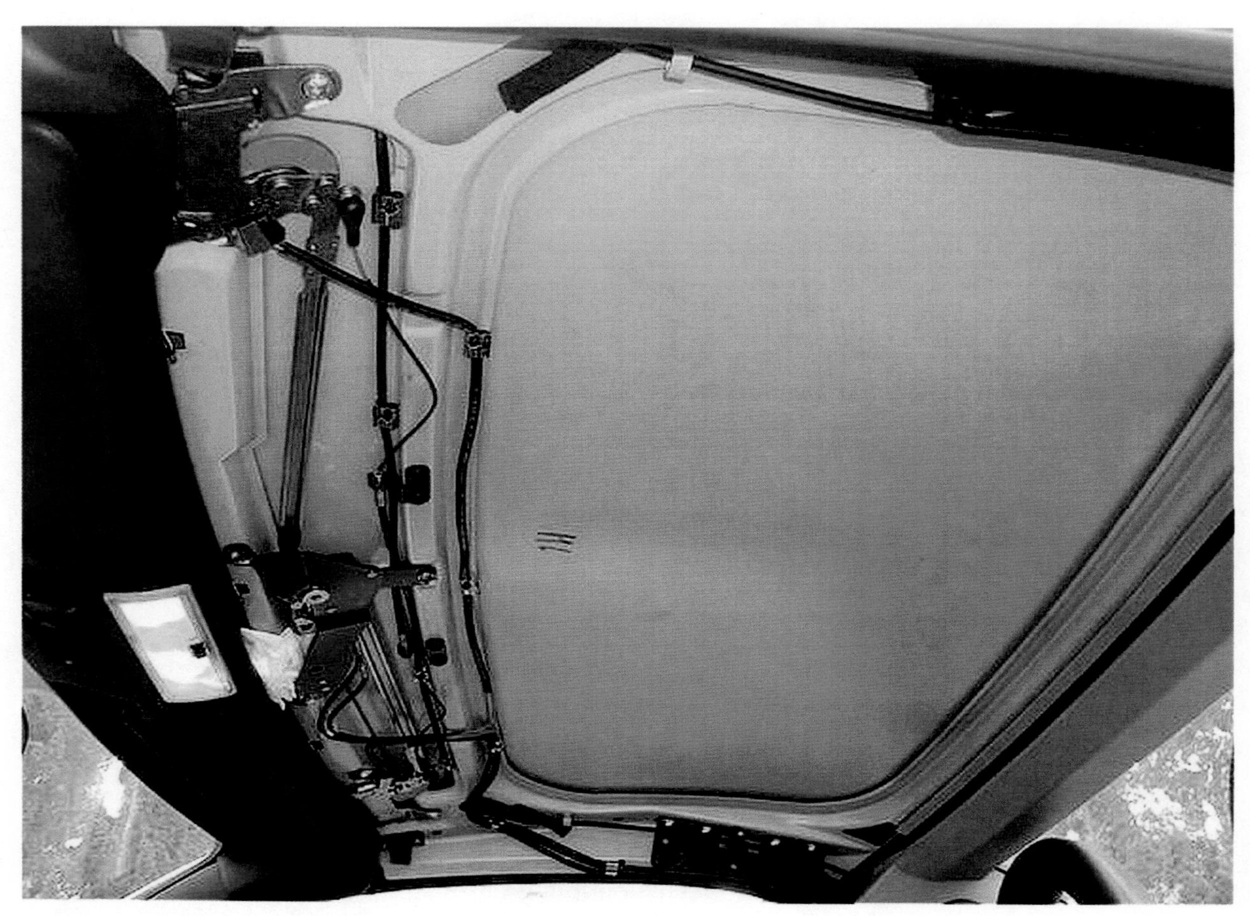

The top with the headliner removed

An interesting way to "upgrade" part of the cover in 300SLR style like with the first prototype

Other sites that cater to all Mercedes models and also the SLK are *http://mbworld.org* and *http://benzworld.org* in the US and in the UK: *www.mbclub.co.uk*. In order to participate in their forums (fora), one needs to register.

The SLK R170

BMW's Z3, a natural rival to the SLK, debuted in autumn 1995. Hot on its heels, the series-production_SLK R170 would star at the spring 1996 Turin auto show, and Porsche answered that with barely a pause, exciting the market even further with the first Boxster in August 1996.

It seemed that after the Mazda Miata was lobbed into the sports-car marketplace, every car manufacturer wanted to have piece of the small or mid-sized open sports car market. While the Miata had created a convertible frenzy among manufacturers, the SLK achieved this with its retractable hardtop. A few years later, around half of all convertibles would be offered with the same technology.

At first glance the SLK (SLK200 internal code: 170.435, SLK230 Kompressor internal code: 170.447) looked almost like the second concept car, but upon more thorough inspection it was evident that there were quite some differences.

The overall dimensions remained unchanged, which meant that the car was not much bigger than the Miata. On the outside, the aluminum look of the front grille had given way to a more traditional SL look with the three-pointed star still prominently in its center. Designed to maximize engine cooling without sacrificing aero-dynamics, the grille featured rows of intake portals that decreased in diameter from the center of the grille to the sides, allowing the maximum amount of cool air to enter where it was needed most. The lower grille opening had fog lights installed at its outer ends. The rollover bars lost their 300SLR look-alike rear cover, as the vario-roof had to be accommodated. Most of the outer panels had been revised a bit, without losing the SLK's sporty, slightly aggressive looking touch. The emotional, almost sexy feeling the concept cars had conveyed, was luckily preserved. The taillights had lost their slightly round appearance and resembled now the ones of the C-class.

As was common practice with Daimler-Benz, the new convertible showed the same rigidity and sturdiness as any Mercedes sedan. Both front and rear had seen a couple of structural steel enforcements, also the A-pillar and gearbox tunnel were considerably strengthened. Both doors were equipped with reinforcement tubes. A similar tube was positioned below the instrument panel. Reinforcements were also used above the rear wall and underneath the seats in order to protect the longitudinal side members.

At a press presentation at the Turin auto show. The show car had highly polished alloys that did not make it into series production

The high-strength rollover bars were bolted to the cross members, which connected the B-pillar stubs. A second wall behind the seats was made of magnesium and positioned between fuel tank and trunk for additional safety and stability. It was the first time that Daimler-Benz had used this material in a structurally relevant part of a production vehicle. Magnesium has half the weight of steel and is also lighter than aluminum with the added advantage of being more rigid (but also more expensive). Magnesium was also used for the cylinder-head covers and the two-part tonneau behind the rollover bars.

Modern cars need to be light enough to save on fuel, yet safe and rigid enough to offer passengers the utmost protection in case of an accident. Some manufacturers such as Audi used (and use) aluminum in their more expensive automobiles to achieve this goal, while Daimler-Benz used "intelligent" steel, which was high strength steel-aluminum that was lighter than standard steel, without compromising on rigidity. In the SLK, one third of all steel used was of the high-strength variety. It helped to ensure that the car's curb weight was only 1,365 kg (3,003 lbs), despite its vario roof and extensive safety features.

The SLK with its ancestor

SLK 230

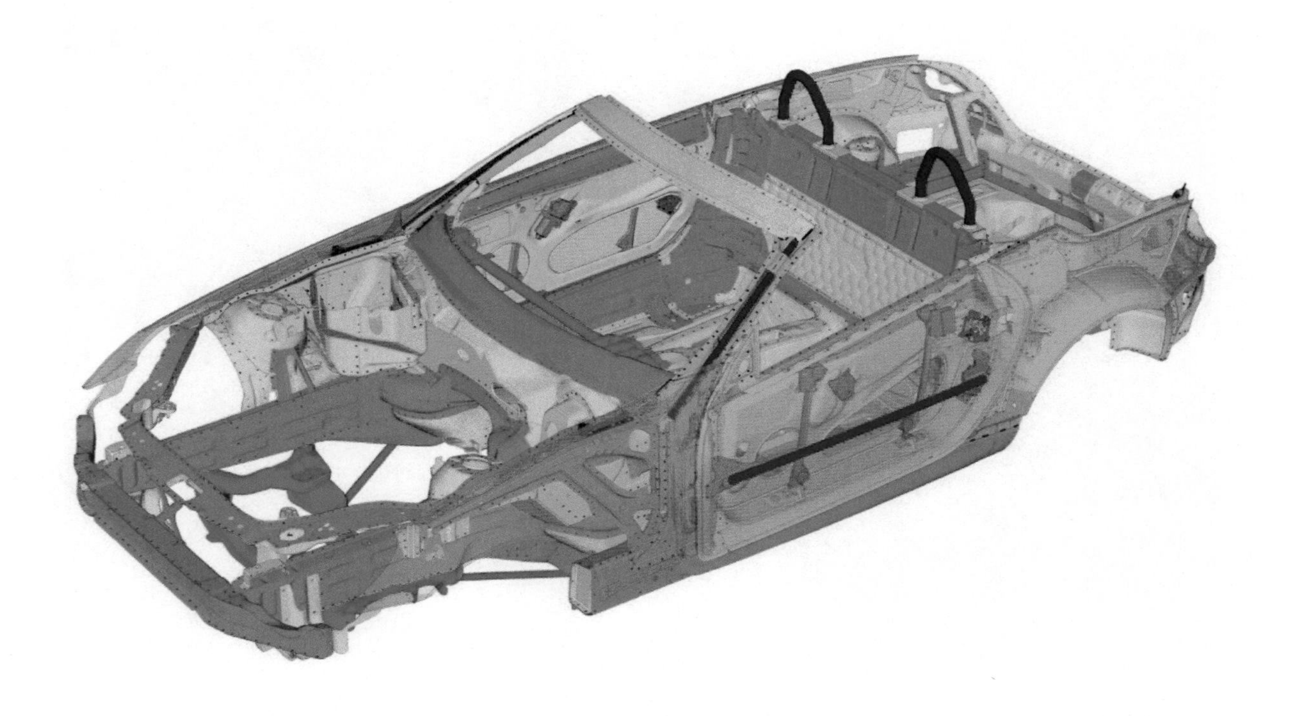

Some forty percent of the body shell is made from high-strength steel (orange)

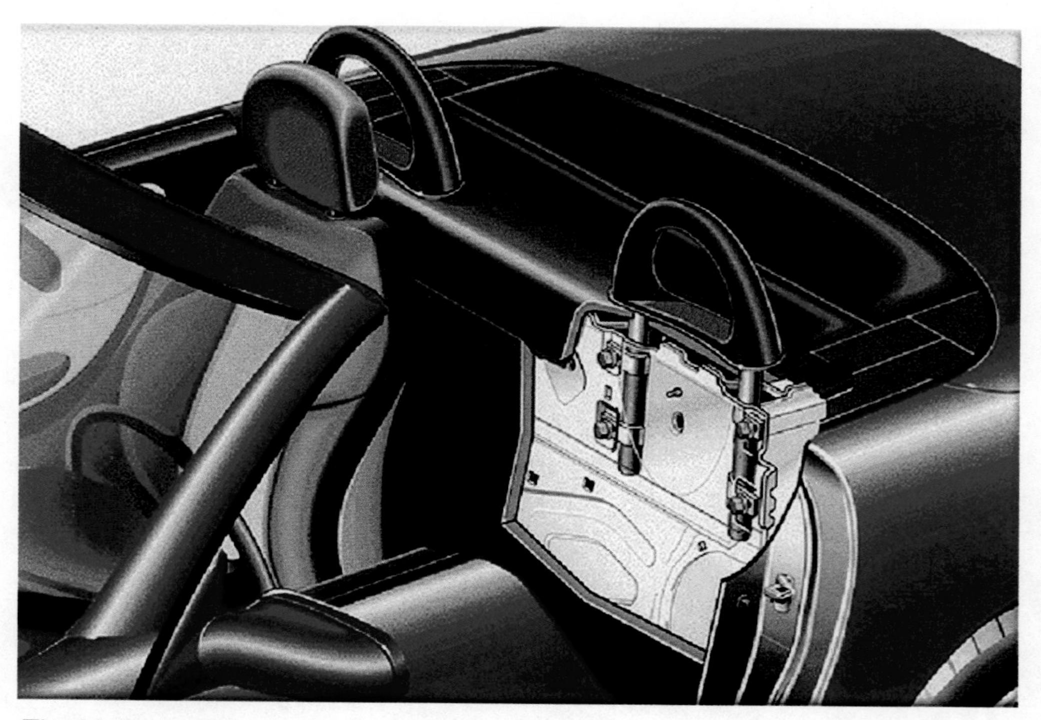

The high-strength steel roll over bars are bolted to the cross-member that connects both B-pillar stubs

Both front and rear axle came from the C-class, with independent double wishbones at the front and a five-arm multilink axle at the rear. The rear suspension was connected to each wheel via five separate flexibly mounted links, which limited the wheel to five possible tracks of movement. The result optimized handling, as the rear wheels were guided with increased precision.

Coil springs, gas pressure shocks, anti-roll bars and anti-dive/anti-lift geometry came from the same W202 C-class source. The coil springs were made stiffer and pre-compressed by 20 mm with a total travel of 195 mm at the front and 205 mm at the rear. This way the SLK provided a good balance between sports car handling and comfort.

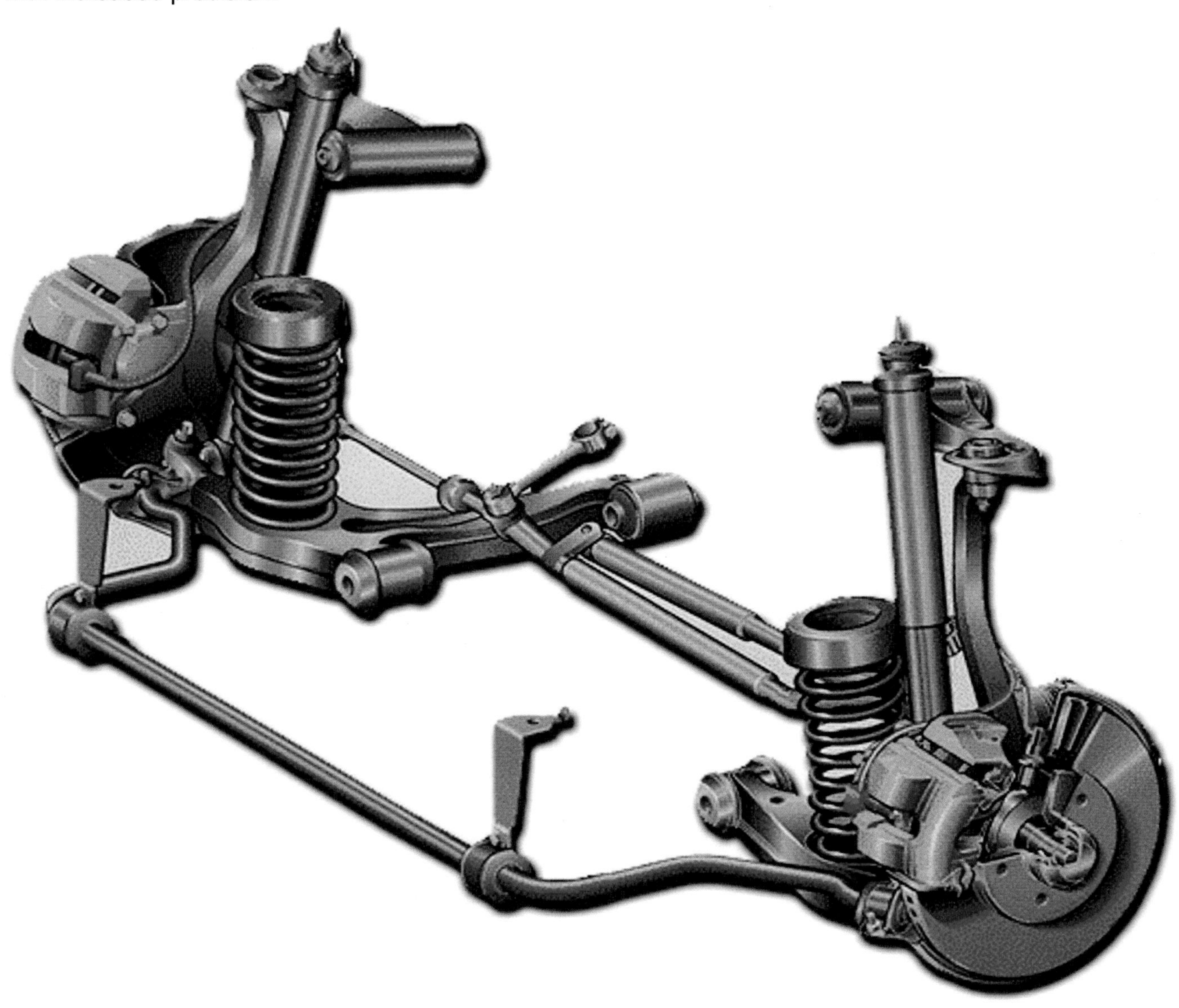

The SLK front axle with independent double wishbones

Shock absorbers and coil springs were positioned separately, so that the shocks did not have to assist guiding the wheels and thus were not subjected to any bending stresses. This had the benefit that they could be tuned more precisely and were as a result more responsive than if operating inside the springs.

Unlike the concept car, the new SLK rested on a shortened version of the C-class platform and offered its re-circulating ball steering system with a relatively direct three turns lock-to-lock. However, it needed to be modified to suit SLK specific parameters. The drag link for example had been changed to suit the reduced track and engine location, which was further aft to ensure a balanced weight distribution. Yet some drivers felt it was a bit uninspiring for such a sports vehicle. It came with power assist and a hydraulic damper.

Both front and rear (above) suspension were borrowed from the C-class

The power assisted ABS brake components had been taken from the E-class with ventilated rotors at the front and solid ones at the back. The Brake Assist system, traction control and an adjustable steering column were, except on a few early cars, standard on all SLK's. The more powerful SLK230 also had the Acceleration Skid Control ASR as standard equipment. It could be manually deactivated. Front discs had a diameter of 287 mm (11.3 in), while the rear diameter was 280 mm (11.0 in). The parking brake lever was no longer installed underneath the dashboard as in the sedans, but in the center console. It was not self-adjusting, so after repair work on the brake, it needed to be adjusted again.

The SLK230 came standard with newly designed 7J x 16 H2 ET37 (front) and 8J x 16 H2 ET30 (rear) light alloy wheels with 205/55 R16 91V tires at the front and 225/50 R16 92V tires at the rear. Daimler-Benz obviously recognized that the short-wheelbase car at stock ride-height could be somewhat nervous under certain driving conditions. So they tried to redress the balance by fitting wider tires at the rear.

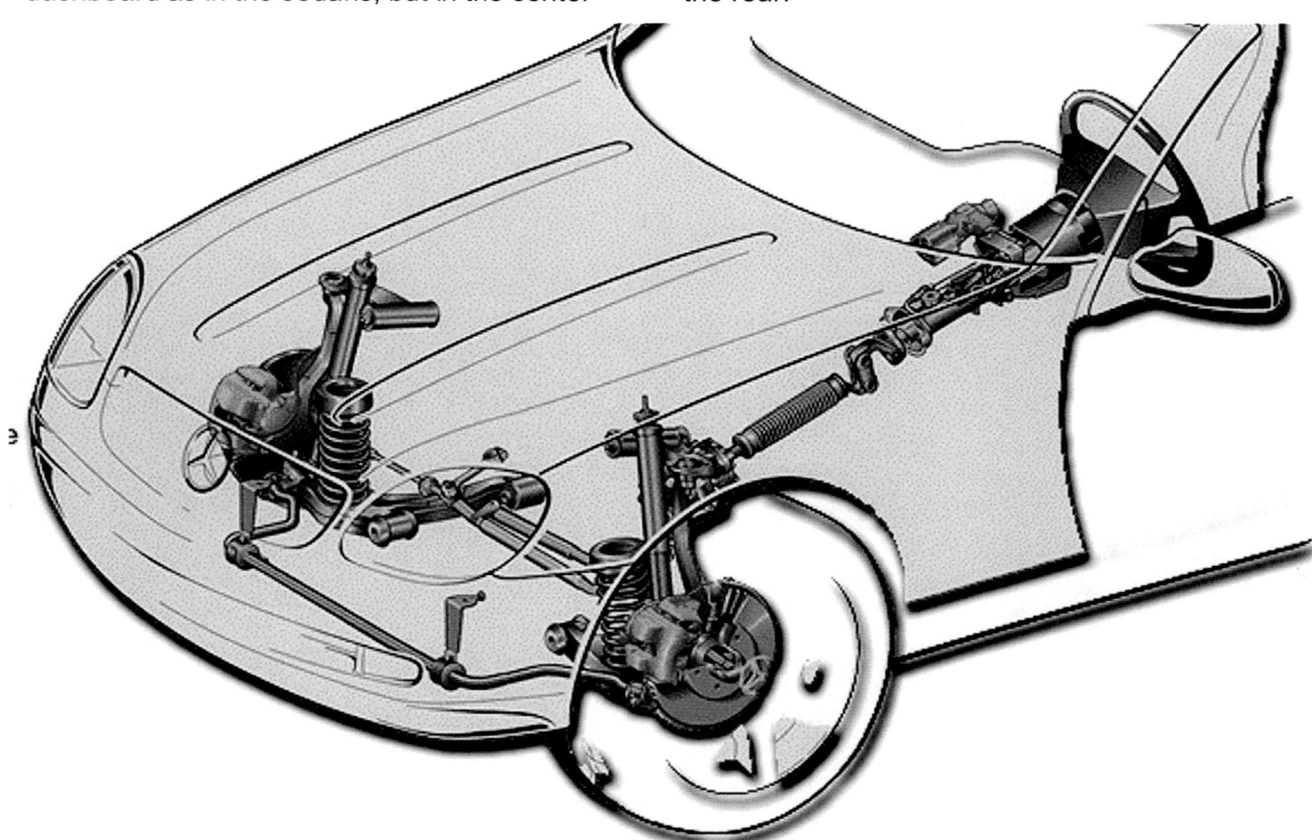

The re-circulating steering was occasionally criticized for its indirect handling characteristics in fast corners

This issue seemed to be less apparent with the SLK200, so it used 205/60 HR 15 tires front and rear. But the larger SLK230 tires were optional. The SLK alloy rims could not be used on the heavier W202 and W210 sedans. Summer tires were supplied by Dunlop (SP Sport 2000E) and Michelin (HX MXM), winter tires by Continental (Winter Contact TS770). ESP was optional for both of these initial SLK variants

Due to the folding top and the car`s compact size, there was no room in the trunk for a traditional spare tire. The SLK came in some markets with a collapsible tire and an electric air pump to inflate it. Its benefit was not only its more compact size but also that it weighed some 30% less than a standard tire. After usage it could be deflated again, but in case of damage it could not be repaired. Both tire and pump could be found together with the jack and wheel wrench under the trunk floor.

For other markets or to customer's specification, the SLK had a TireFit repair set instead, which had been developed by Dunlop. The fuel tank offered 53 l (12 gallons), which should be enough for 500 km of travel.

The Dunlop TireFit repair kit left room for an additional small luggage piece

The interior of the SLK had seen the biggest changes when compared with the concept vehicles. The lightness of the first dashboard had given way to a more traditional (safer), yet still fashionable looking Daimler-Benz interpretation. Elegant looking instruments with polished aluminum rims had an ivory fascia and red needle pointers, just like in the days of the famous 1930s Silver Arrows.

A maintenance indicator was integrated into the digital display field of the odometer. It came on some 3,000 km or 30 days prior to the due date for the next maintenance. The remaining days or mileage could also be pulled up manually any time by turning the ignition key to position two and then press the button on the left of the tachometer within four seconds.

Later SLK models with miles speedo did not have the km markings

The SLK came with an innovative back-lighting concept, adapted from the SL

The leather wrapped steering wheel was a new design with separate horn buttons that came from the SL, which used it since 1995. However, for the SLK its diameter was reduced to 380 mm. Seats were manually adjustable with eight-way electrically movable seats as an option. In some markets, the seats came standard with fabric upholstery.

Its design was called "Caruso". But hardly any SLKs were delivered with these. Full leather trim was standard only in North America (heated seats were optional for all markets). For comparison: the old 190SL was offered standard in the first years with MB-Tex. When looking at interior color options, it became clear that the SLK was aimed at a different, younger clientele than other Mercedes models. There were five solid tones (red, green, beige, black and blue) and three two-tone leather color choices available.

No SL had such options ever (except for the later introduced "Designo" versions). The top of the dashboard, steering wheel and the sides of the seats were colored in anthracite, while the rest, such as dashboard, center console, door panels and gearshift leather offered the color of the seats.

Rare "Caruso"-design fabric seats. They were also available in blue, red and green

Most cars came equipped with a single tone leather interior

Given the younger average age of SLK drivers (compared with the average SL owner), two-tone leather seats were popular

Dashboard and center console were color-coordinated with the leather interior and gave the car a fresh, youthful appeal

Seat cushions and backrests were designed as all-foam cushions. Steel spring cores were history. This became necessary, as thickly padded steel spring seats could not have been accommodated in the tight cabin. In order to maximize the passengers' comfort, the seats offered a new suspension approach, which was called the Swing-Seat system. The cushion, which rested in a plastic tray, pivoted at the front on a shaft, while it was supported at the rear by two springs. The seat adjustment was supported by a gas pressure strut. When the height of the seat was changed, the seat cushions inclination was now also automatically adjusted. The headrests could only be adjusted in height, they could not be rotated fore and aft.

Other goodies included cruise control, simulated carbon fiber applications, power mirrors, door-locks and windows. A high performance AM/FM cassette stereo with six-speaker Bose sound system (CD changer was optional) and a draft blocker, which fit over the roll bars, came standard. CFC free air-conditioning with dual-zone temperature controls was at least for North America also part of the standard equipment.

Dual zone air-con was standard in North America, Australia and Japan, but not Europe

The climate control system was similar to the one in the W210 E-class. But as there was no in-car temperature sensor as in the E-class, the SLK system controlled the temperature only at the air outlets. A dust and pollen filter was standard. The optional CD changer was part of a package, called K1. It included an integrated cellular telephone along with the CD changer and cost $1,595.

The standard remote-control key was equipped with a new "Drive Authorization System" DAS that should ensure better operating reliability. While previous systems were armed or disarmed by an infra-red remote control, DAS relied on data transfer from the ignition block. The remote key now had a transponder with an automatic code modulator built-in. The transponder sourced its energy from a coil on the ignition lock, when the ignition was switched on. This triggered a signal, which was then received by the coil and transmitted to the central locking unit. If this unit recognized the code to be correct, it sent a signal to the engine management, which in turn allowed the power plant to be started. The advantage of the new system was that it did not rely anymore on the key`s properly charged battery to function, as it did not require that battery's power.

A cellular phone and CD changer were part of the K1 package

The CD changer, mounted in the trunk, could not be ordered separately

The key also offered two different function modes, one was the "selective", the other the "global" mode. In selective mode, the remote button would unlock the driver's door and fuel filler flap. Pressed twice also the trunk would be unlocked. In global mode, all three would be unlocked at the same time.

A feature that was advanced for its time was the airbag system with dual front and optional side-impact bags. The passenger airbag would not deploy with less than a 12 kg (25 lbs) downforce on the passenger seat. Also when the optional BabySmart child seat was installed, the passenger airbag was automatically deactivated.

The first SLKs came out in Germany in July 1996, although pre-production cars had been sent to dealers or were already being used internally since mid-November 1995. Other European markets received their cars around autumn 1996/spring 1997, although an exception seems to be Monte Carlo, as a few SLKs became available there as early as April 1996. US models hit American showrooms in autumn 1997 as 1998 models. Hard-core driving enthusiasts, who had expected a true sports car, quickly complained about uninspiring handling caused by the outdated re-circulating ball steering set-up and questionable sporting credentials. It was also noted that interior space was limited. There was hardly room for a road-atlas or even a coat. But the emotional side in the prospective owner could not care less.

The interior offered just enough space to store maps or documents

The SLK looked well proportioned, particularly given the awkward engineering problems thrown up by folding hardtops. When asked at the car's presentation, who would be the prospective buyer, Daimler-Benz managers answered that they expected a younger audience between 30 and 40. At least half of them would be women. They also hoped to lure at least thirty percent from other brands, BMW in particular. At least in the US the buyer demographics did not work out as planned though, because this sporty looking, youthful two-door fun car was bought predominantly (seven out of ten) by male baby-boomers and retirees. Most of them had owned a Mercedes before and were drawn by the car's great looks and its novel roof mechanism. As one early owner wrote: "The technical design of my new toy is nothing short of fantastic. I enjoy the way people stare, when they see the SLK change itself from a coupe to a sun-loving cabriolet." When people previously saw a new sports car, they wanted to know from the lucky owner the horsepower or how fast the car could drive. With the SLK most wanted to see a little demonstration of the roof. The buyers' demographic issue was a bit different in Europe, as some 42 percent of first time SLK buyers came from other car brands.

The US magazine *Car and Driver* said in its January 1997 issue: "*We've seen supercharged engines before. We've seen carbon-fiber interior panels. We've even seen folding steel convertible tops before. But we've never seen these features, and more, wrapped in a lovely, agile package adorned with the three-pointed star on its hood….the SLK defines a new paradigm for sports cars—one that rivals will be chasing in the forthcoming years.*" It was no surprise that the car was on the magazine's Ten Best List for 1997 and was named "North American Car of the Year" in 1998.

At the time of its launch, Italian journalists were convinced that the SLK was the "*most beautiful car in the world*", The British *Car Magazine* hailed it as the "*Best Technical Concept*" and presented head of Daimler-Benz design Bruno Sacco at the Birmingham Motor Show 1996 with a design award. The German *Bild am Sonntag* newspaper awarded the SLK the "Golden Steering Wheel". This continued in 1997, where the car received 20 international awards. Even in 1999, three years after its launch, it still harvested three international prizes.

The four-cylinder engines

The SLK was geared towards a clientele that was not really interested in what Daimler-Benz otherwise had to offer. Being mostly younger than the traditional Mercedes customer, the SL was for many out of their financial reach and the reliable sedans not really their preference. The SLK would hopefully bring them into the fold, and Daimler-Benz was naturally concerned with what engines to offer. Daimler-Benz was not exactly famous for offering cars for the masses, so in order to appeal to a larger audience they needed an entry-level engine that gave the SLK owners the brand name and the looks, but not necessarily the performance. It was the same philosophy Ford had used when launching the first Mustang or Opel and Ford in Europe with the introduction of their popular Manta and Capri sports cars.

In came the 2.0L M111 E20 with just 136 hp. That was not really the engine to, as the SLK brochure enticed, "unleash the sporting talent". Due to its price, though, the least powerful SLK power plant became quite popular in those markets where it was made available. And that success was exactly what Daimler-Benz had anticipated.

The modest inline four-cylinder engine (internal code: 111.946) had been introduced first in 1992 in the W124 E-class. When it was developed, engineers wanted to create a power plant that was not only quiet but, for its small displacement, also powerful at low engine speeds. It was the first mass-produced Mercedes engine that used four valves per cylinder. This system had been seen on their four-cylinder cars only with the predecessor engine M102 for the low volume 190E 2.3-16 and 190E 2.5-16. With a bore of 89.9 mm and a stroke of 78.7 mm it was an over-square design, which used a cast iron engine block and an aluminum alloy cylinder head.

The M111 developed its maximum output at 5,500 rpm and offered its maximum torque of 190 NM (140.1 ft-lbs) between 3,700 and 4,500 rpm, meaning it wanted to be pushed to deliver performance in the good old Uhlenhaut fashion of the 1960s. Contrary to what engineers had in mind during its creation, there was not much to write home about at anything below 2,000 rpm. This was probably fine with the average E-class driver, but not necessarily with the somewhat more power hungry SLK driver. Consequently this engine was never available in the US and UK.

The 2.0 L engine was not exported to the UK and US

In this respect the M111 was actually fairly similar to the old 190SL (internally sometimes called the "rattle king" because of its engine noise), which offered its 142 NM (104.7 ft-lbs) at 3,200 rpm. Other performance data of the new SLK200 were its top speed of 208 km/h (129 mph) and an acceleration of 9.3 seconds from 0 to 100 km/h. During the days of the 190SL, this was almost 300SL territory.

But for the more power-hungry, help was on its way - things looked much brighter with the inline-four-cylinder 2.3 L DOHC four-valve-per-cylinder engine. It used a belt-driven Roots-type Eaton M62 compressor or supercharger with an air-to-air intercooler. The compressor was driven by a separate belt directly from the crankshaft. Two three-lobed rotors, set at an angle of 60 degrees to each other and coated with epoxy for greater efficiency, rotated without touching inside a housing, forcing the inlet air out through the opposite outlet port. The compressor did not run permanently though, as this would have drawn too much power away from the engine. An electromagnetic coupling, which was controlled by the engine management system, engaged the compressor only in the upper part-load and full-load range.

The engine was equipped with a new Bosch Motronik engine management system ME 2.1. On top of controlling fuel injection ignition and anti-knocking, it also monitored the position of electronic accelerator pedal, cruise control and drive authorization.

The 2.3 L supercharged engine was praised for its low rev pull and power

With 193 hp (185 hp for the US) at 5,300 rpm the engine (M 111 E23 ML, internal code: 111.973) offered quite a spirited performance. Its maximum torque of 280 NM (206.5 ft-lbs) was available from 2,500 to 4,800 rpm, which meant the car did not need to be revved as much as the naturally aspirated SLK200 in order to offer sufficient performance. It could achieve a top speed of 231 km/h (144 mph) with an acceleration of 7.4 seconds. Unfortunately the 2.3 L engine was a bit notorious for vibrations at higher rpm and had a rather dull, almost anemic exhaust note.

Daimler-Benz reacted to such complains and offered later a special AMG end-muffler in order to facilitate a somewhat deeper sound. The 2.0 L engine did not sound much better, but at least it had fewer vibrations. In Europe, both engines were mated as standard to a five-speed manual gearbox. Only in North America and the UK was the 2.3 L car offered as standard with a five-speed electronically controlled automatic box. Launched in 1990, it featured as a technical novelty a driver-adaptive shift logic, which simply meant that it automatically deferred to a higher shifting point, when it detected more engaged driving behavior.

Officially named 722.6, the auto box was also capable of changing shifting points, when driving on mountainous roads. A lock-up torque converter engaged in third, fourth and fifth gear in order to increase the car's fuel efficiency. It all sounded terribly convincing on paper, yet despite all its technical virtues, some drivers complained that the auto box did not seem to be smart enough to know what the driver wanted. It shifted nervously in combination with the supercharged engine and was from time to time in the wrong gear, especially when cornering. But at least it pushed the car from 0 to 100 km/h in 0.1 seconds faster than the manual car. In 2003, this transmission was to be replaced by the 7G-Tronic 722.9.

South European markets such as Portugal, Italy and Greece did not get the 2.3 L engine, as high taxes for engine displacements over 2.0 L would have made the car too expensive. Instead, a somewhat stretched 2.0 L supercharged engine (M111 E20 ML, internal code 111.943) was offered that delivered 192 hp at 5,300 rpm - the same (bar a single horsepower) as its bigger cousin. Its maximum torque of 270 NM (199.1 ft-lbs), a mere 10 NM off, was available over the same wide band of 2,500 rpm to 4,800 rpm. The SLK200 Kompressor had the internal code 170.444.

The "Kompressor" cars had that name proudly displayed on both front fenders, making it the first supercharged Mercedes since the days of the glorious 500K and 540K from the 1930s. While the final drive ratio for the SLK200 was 3.91:1 for both manual and automatic transmissions, the manual SLK230 came with a 3.46, the automatic car with a 3.27 ratio.

In the US the SLK230 went on sale for $41,300, while in the UK it cost some £26,500. In Germany it was available at DM 60,950 ($41,250 at contemporary exchange rate). That was less than half of what the SL cost. Only one year later prices in Germany rose to DM 62,560. The SLK200 with manual transmission cost in Germany DM 52,900, while it became available in the UK only in 2000 as a facelift model in supercharged form. As already stated, it was never officially sold in the US.

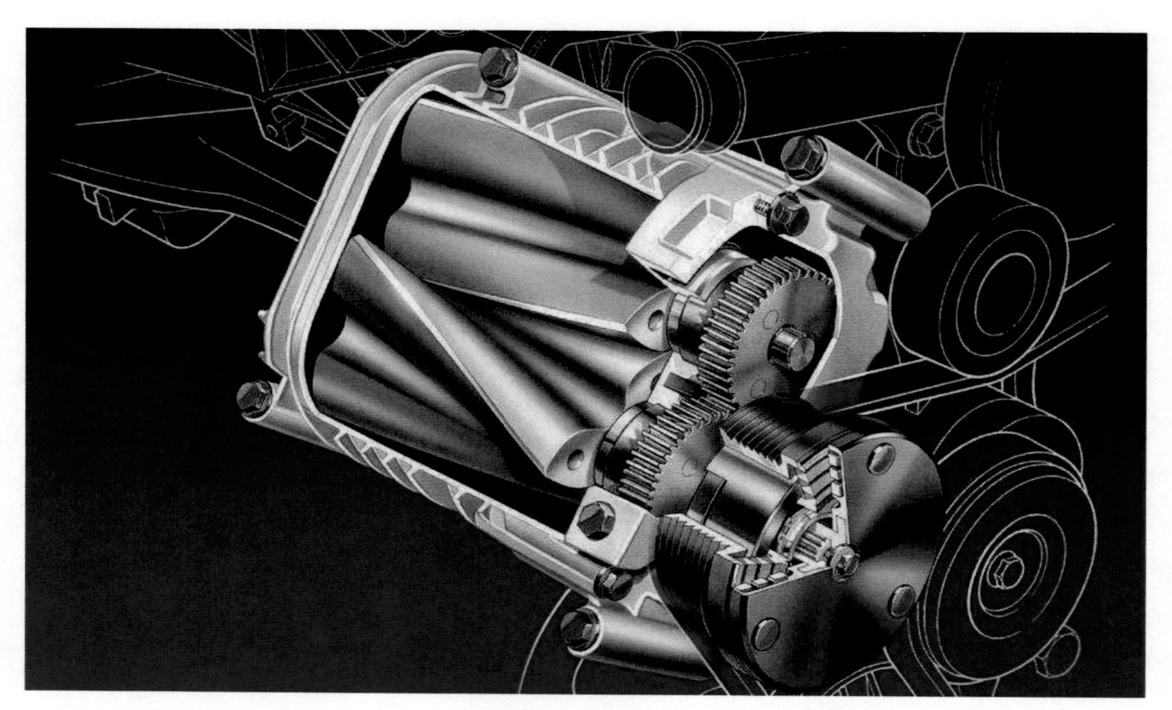

A look inside the kompressor and fuel direct-injection of the SLK230K (below)

First upgrades

UK and North American automotive journalists had complained that "their" SLKs did not have the manual transmission, so in 1998 that was changed. Daimler-Benz estimated though that not more than just twenty percent of all cars would be ordered that way. That estimate proved to be accurate. Two other interesting options became also available that year: the AMG Sport Package and the Designo-Line. The "SP1 Sport Package" called AMG option provided a more masculine and aerodynamic appearance of the car's lower body. The enhancements could be seen at the bumpers and side-sills and included different projector beam front fog lamps. It also came with beefier 17-in tires: 225/45 ZR 17 at the front and 245/40 ZR 17 at the rear with AMG five-spoke monoblock alloys. Those wider tires made the car handle even better, as if it wanted to swallow the pavement before it would cave in and start to slide.

To make sure that everybody knew that the AMG package was installed, the "Kompressor" badge on the front fenders was replaced with the word "Sport". The "Kompressor" badge did not disappear though, it still showed up on the trunk lid. In the US the AMG package cost $4,050.-, while it was available in Europe at €6,900.- w/o VAT.

The Kompressor badge was replaced by a "Sport" badge

The AMG sport package was especially popular in the US

Special five-spoke AMG alloys cost an additional €5,500 w/o VAT

The Kompressor sign moved to the trunk

Ever conscious of its buyers' fashion leanings, Daimler-Benz used its Designo-Line to offer special colors along with unique interior trims. Initially just two options were added, the first one being the "Copper Edition". It featured a copper metallic paint and an interior that was finished in copper and two-tone charcoal leather. Steering wheel, shift knob, floor mats, center console and rollover bars also received the copper and charcoal trim.

The copper edition had two-tone charcoal seat trim

The second Designo SLK was called "Electric Green" and used charcoal leather and trim in combination with light green. Other interior options were Oyster/Charcoal and Salsa/Charcoal combinations. Also a solid Charcoal version was made available. The Designo-Line theme proved to be quite popular (and profitable for Daimler-Benz), so it was to be extended further with the face lifted models.

The interior remained otherwise unchanged, only the stereo with cassette player was a new generation version that used fiber-optic technology and offered integrated controls for a cell phone.

Daimler-Benz mentioned in a US ad that the 1999 SLK only had five factory options: automatic transmission ($900), metallic paint ($600), heated seats ($595), Motorola phone with CD changer ($1,595) and the somewhat pricey, but very good looking AMG Sport Package ($ 3,990). This reflected the preferences of the North American SLK buyer. That they thought it was worth mentioning showed what image the company had with its customers. Marketing and Sales had studied their potential clientele quite well. Those "youngsters" did not like to flip through endless lists of pricey extras. They were used to have most of it in one not too costly package. It was a welcome change from the usual habit of Daimler-Benz and other German manufacturers to charge for goodies that Japanese manufacturers, for example, offered as standard equipment. And that the Florida retiree suddenly saw it hip to be seen in such a great car too, must have been an unplanned, but certainly not unwanted bonus.

Unfortunately the company thought otherwise about its European clientele, where with a few exceptions the options-list was as long as ever and extras needed to be paid for.

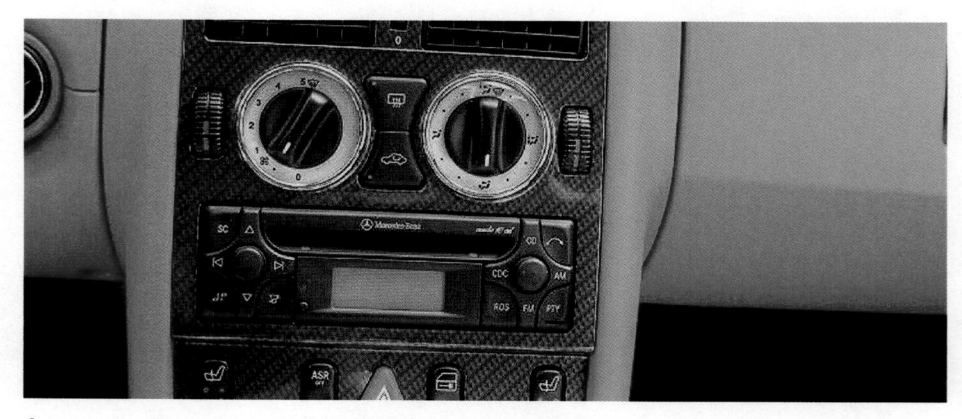

A new audio system with optional in-dash CD player was introduced

"Electric Green" was the second Designo option

A fitting interior was two-tone green (code X52)

The 2000 facelift

Four- and six-cylinder engines and chassis:

The year 2000, the fourth year after the SLK's introduction, saw the first major revision. Press photos of the face-lifted cars became available starting December 2nd 1999, while the car was first shown on January 4th 2000 at the Detroit Motor Show. European customers would see the car first on Jan. 18th in Bruxelles, Belgium. Pre-production started on February 1st, with production of the first cars for customers starting March 11th at the Bremen plant (which also produced the SL R129). On March 18th, the first production batch of the updated car was shipped to dealers. In the US, where the car became available shortly thereafter, it would be sold as a 2001 model.

Although the naturally aspirated SLK200 sold quite well in markets, where it was available, Daimler-Benz felt at the end that 136 hp might not be good enough in a sports car. Another, possibly more important, reason could have been that they wanted the SLK not to be in the same power league as the much cheaper Mazda Miata, which offered since 1998 a 1.8 L engine with 140 hp. In came a new SLK200 Kompressor (internal code: 170.445) with a healthier 163 hp at 5,300 rpm. It also replaced the previous supercharged SLK200. Its engine (M111 E20 ML Evo, internal code: 111.958) developed like the 2.3 L supercharged engine its maximum torque of 230 NM (169.6 ft-lbs) over an impressively wide band from 2,500 to 4,800 rpm. The car achieved a top speed of 223 km/h (138.6 mph) and accelerated from 0 to 100 km/h of 8.4 seconds. That was just one second slower than the SLK230.

With the SLK200 revitalized, it was felt that the 2.3 L engine of the SLK230 Kompressor (170.449) could also do with a bit more verve. The compression was increased from 8.8 to 9.0:1, the cylinder head optimized and the exhaust system slightly altered for easier breathing. Now the engine offered 197 hp at 5,500 rpm (previously 193 at 5,300 rpm). In the US, the car was rated at 192 hp. The maximum torque remained the same, but was useable up to 5,000 rpm (previously 4,800 rpm).

The top speed increased from 231 to 240 km/h (from 143.5 to 149.1 mph), while acceleration was now 7.2 instead of 7.4 seconds. The internal engine code changed from 111.973 to 111.983.

Finally the SLK200 received a supercharged engine for all markets. This version also replaced the old 200 Kompressor version for southem Europe

The M111 E20 ML Evo became also available in the UK, but not North America

The 2.3 L received a few more horsepower, but was left otherwise unchanged

The micro-processor-controlled fuel injection used in the pre-facelift SLK230, as already mentioned earlier, was a Bosch Motronic type ME 2.1 (SLK200: MSE from VDO, SLK200 Kompressor also Bosch ME 2.1). Both engines received now a Siemens Motronic SIM 4 LE. The SLK230 also received newly styled six-spoke alloy wheels. The dimensions remained the same with 7J x 16 and tire size 205/55-16 at the front and 8J x 16 with 225/50-16 at the rear.

They were optionally available again for the base SLK, which came standard despite its more powerful engine with seven-spoke 7J x 15 alloys and 205/60-15 tires front and rear.

The exhaust tip on both cars featured an elegant looking chrome cover.

The best news though was the announcement that the long hoped for 3.2 L (195 cu in) engine that already powered many other Mercedes models, would be made available in the SLK. The 3.2 L M112 engine was interesting, as it was the first V6 engine Daimler-Benz had ever produced. Around 500 engineers were in one way or another part of the development and it took over 400 test engines, until the result was to their satisfaction. To enable it to fit into the engine bay, it was necessary to move the steering box.

The new location was also adopted for the other SLK models. Daimler-Benz knew of the criticism that the four-cylinder engines did not provide the sound people wanted to hear in a sports car. Therefore, the new engine came with a special exhaust system that should orchestrate the typical sound of a powerful six-cylinder.

Built in the engine manufacturing plant in Bad Cannstatt, which is some 5 km north of Stuttgart, the new power plant had a 90 degrees V-angle aluminum engine block with aluminum/silicon lined cylinders. 90 degree V-angle engines were known for their vibration issues at certain loads, so a balancer shaft was installed in the engine block between the cylinder banks, which should cause a few issues in the next SLK generation.

The new M112 3.2 L engine

The M112 V6 installed in the SLK320

The integrated sequential multipoint fuel injection with Bosch ME 2.8 Motronic came with two spark plugs per cylinder for maximum combustion. The SOHC cylinder heads had three valves per cylinder, two intake and one exhaust valve. Other features were forged steel connecting rods, one-piece cast camshafts, iron-coated aluminum pistons and a magnesium intake manifold. In order to increase engine flexibility under load, a dual-length variable length intake manifold was fitted.

This M112 E32 power plant (internal code: 112.947) was built in five versions from 2.6 to 3.7 L, one of them being the 3.2 L AMG variant. All versions had a bore of 89.9 mm, the 3.2 L engine was stroked to 84 mm and offered in the sedans an output from 218 to 224 hp at 5,700 rpm. One of the differences between this power plant and the four-cylinder versions was the fracture-split forged steel connecting rods it contained.

The SLK320 (170.465) offered 218 hp at 5,700 rpm (215 hp in the US) with a 10.0:1 compression ratio. That was the same output as in the new W203 C320 and the CLK320. A maximum torque of 310 NM (228.6 ft-lbs), available from 3,000 to 4,600 rpm, combined with a much better sounding six-cylinder growl, guaranteed a broad grin on the driver's face in almost all situations. And a top speed of 245 km/h (152 mph) plus an acceleration of just 6.9 seconds made the car a true member of the elite sports car club. Especially as the curb weight from SLK230 to SLK320 had only increased by a mere 20 kg from 1,385 kg to 1,405 kg (3,091 lbs). The SLK320 was the only Mercedes-Benz in which this superb six-cylinder powerhouse was available with manual transmission.

The SLK320 had a unique front apron design

The front brake discs were enlarged from 287 mm to 300 mm in order to cope with the increased performance. The rear diameter remained at 279.4 mm. The SLK320 came also with unique 16 inch five-spoke alloy wheels, while carrying the SLK230 tires. It also had a slightly different lower air-intake in the front bumper to distinguish it from its cheaper cousins.

All models received a fuel tank that was enlarged from 53 L (12 gallons) to 60 L (14 gallons). The engines and exhaust systems of all three models were continuously controlled by a new onboard diagnostic system. It conformed to the latest European EU-4 emission standards and had a small red light in the instrument panel to inform the driver if a component affecting emissions was malfunctioning. Standard on all versions was the Electronic Stability Program ESP and a newly-developed, much-improved six-speed manual transmission with tempomat, called Speedtronic. Cars ordered with the five-speed automatic transmission would also get the so-called *Tipshift.*

While the automatic adapted to the individual driver's style by continuously adjusting its shift points, the driver could now use the tipshift (or TouchShift) to mimic a manual gearbox without having to use a clutch. With the gear selector in position D, one needed to push the lever to the left in order to shift down or to the right to shift up. If the engine was running at high rpms, the automatic would refuse to shift down, as it would detect that this would over-rev and potentially damage the engine.

Except for badge and front apron, the exterior of the SLK320 was identical with those of the smaller versions

Passengers' safety was further increased with side-impact bags in both doors and the addition of the Brake Assist System BAS, which operated in emergency braking situations. If the driver pushed the brake pedal quickly, BAS automatically increased the brake pressure and thus reduced the stopping distance.

The car's unibody structure was further reinforced and the sheet metal of the engine bay's ellipsoid firewall thickened. Impact absorbers were added to the chassis' side members in order to support the wheels in an offset crash. Also a link was added between the car's rear body and main structure in order to disperse rear impacts. Other changes were a reinforced front stabilizer bar and the addition of a stabilizer bar at the rear. Prior to the facelift it had none at the rear. Improved shock absorbers helped to increase dynamic stability and a lower body (by 5 mm) made the car look sportier.

In the US TeleAid became standard on all Mercedes models, including the SLK. The system incorporated remote diagnosis, emergency door unlocking and anti-theft alarm notification. Emergency and non-emergency buttons established voice contact with reception specialists who could then dispatch local police or other services. GPS tracking pinpointed the car's location automatically. This also informed authorities the location of stolen SLKs.

Body and interior:

The body changes were less dramatic, as Daimler-Benz did not want to spoil a proven and well-accepted design. The bumpers received a mild update with integrated spoiler lips. This increased the car's overall length by 15 mm from 3,995 mm to 4,010 mm. In addition, fenders and doorsills saw slight changes. All this resulted in an improved Cd value, which was reduced in case of the SLK200 Kompressor by six percent to 0.33 (0.34 for SLK 230 and 320).

The fog lamps looked like the ones of the S-class coupe and the rearview mirrors adapted from other Mercedes models integrated turn indicators. That meant that the clear-glass indicators in the sides of the front fenders disappeared. The previously matte grille received a glossy coating and the lower air intake was styled more elliptically. Headlights, now with clear-glass indicators, could be ordered with xenon lights, heated headlight washers and dynamic headlight adjuster.

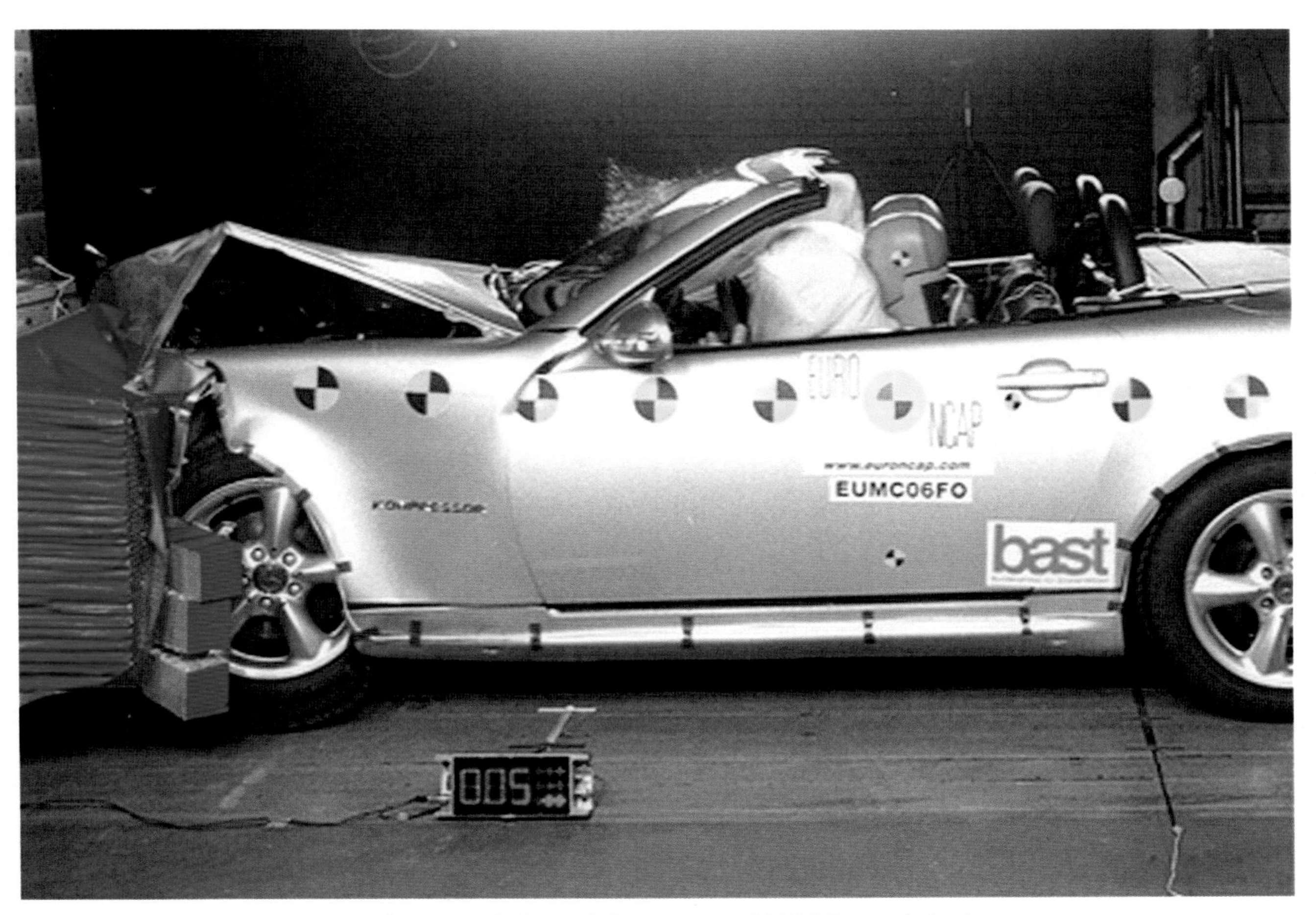

Both body and chassis were further reinforced (here at an ANCAP crash test

The most significant outside difference between "old" and "new" was the missing trunk opener

A change that was not universally appreciated was the trunk opener button, which was located in the pre-facelift cars between license plate and right taillight. Now it was moved under the trunk handle and some owners argued that it was less easy to operate than the old version. The taillights had slightly rounder edges around the small flutes and a mildly revised clear part in the design. All this was supposed to clean up the rear and make it appear wider. The lower portions of front and rear bumpers plus the doorsills and door handles were now painted in the respective body color, so the whole car appeared fresher.

In an effort to suit all possible tastes, the SLK was available in seven solid colors, ten metallic paints and an amazing twenty-two Designo variations. Though not all colors were available in all markets all the time, however, for example in Germany a total of just ten colors were offered. However, this shows how much focus Daimler-Benz gave to fashion and individuality. But it did not stop there. The standard anthracite-grey fabric was changed from a “Caruso” to an “Arezzo” scheme. Next to grey, the Arezzo design was also available in magma-red and merlin-blue.

Xenon headlamps were not yet very common on the R170

The options now included nine new leather colors, among them *merlin-blue*, *siam-beige*, *magma-red* and *lotos-yellow*. Can you imagine these names in those days for an S-class? The Designo options even included twenty-two leather colors to complement the Designo exterior colours. This number actually almost doubled, as most of them were also offered in a two-color combination. Again, not all combinations and colors were offered in all markets. As before, the entire interior was color-coordinated. The chosen color option could be found on not only the seat's surface, but also the inner parts of the door panels, the dashboard, the center console, gearshift lever plus its leather cover and the upper inner parts of the newly designed steering wheel. Another feature, unique to the Designo Line, was a different wood application, called "Cinnamora". It was available in two color tones, "Anthratic" and "Nature light".

The following four photos should give a bit of a demonstration, which color options could be ordered with the Designo line:

SLK32 with two-tone Designo purple (X54) interior

SLK32 AMG with two-tone Designo yellow-gold interior (X69)

SLK320 with two-tone Designo light-brown interior (X63)

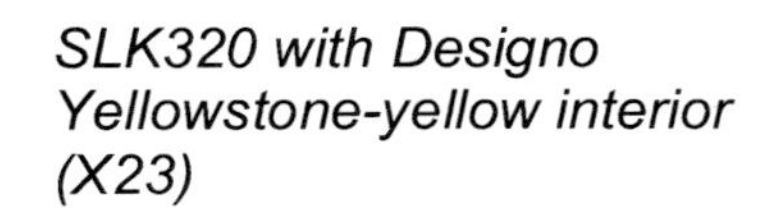

SLK320 with Designo Yellowstone-yellow interior (X23)

In a bow to past criticism the seats were made more durable and ergonomically improved. The SLK320 came standard with eight-way electrically movable seats, which were, as noted, available as an extra for the four-cylinder vehicles. Heated seats were optional for all three cars. Other changes included a different gearshift lever design and metal plate door sills with either SLK or V6 (SLK320) markings. The simulated carbon fiber applications were replaced with machined aluminum trim.

Machined aluminum trim replaced the simulated carbon fiber trim

Dual zone air-con was standard in Europe only in the SLK320

The eucalyptus wood looked equally good with light or dark interior colors

Real wood was available as an option in either eucalyptus wood or blackened birds-eye maple. The eucalyptus wood option was standard in the SLK320 with a combination wood/leather steering wheel and gearshift knob. The maintenance indicator, integrated into the digital display field for the odometer, was enlarged for better visibility. Also a touch-shift indicator was added to the instrument panel. The hand brake received a nice looking chromed button and the door panels looked now similar to the ones in the SL. Dual zone air-conditioning was in most European markets standard only for the SLK320. The UK and North America had it better, as also the SLK230 came equipped with air-con. The previously standard manually adjustable steering column was, for the four-cylinder cars, moved to the options list in all markets.

Pricing for the SLK200 Kompressor started in 2000 in Germany at €30,000 and in the UK at £19,500. The SLK230 Kompressor cost in Germany €33,000, while it was available in the UK for £21,450. In the US the car cost some $42,500. The SLK320 cost in Germany €38,800. In the UK it started at £24,700.-, while it was available in the US at $45,500.-. Those prices increased with the exception of the US over the next years in total by some reasonable five to six percent, until the cars' production was halted in 2004. The days of the early SL R129, where prices had been hiked twice a year, were clearly over. Whether it was due to currency fluctuations or a more challenging competitive situation, it is interesting to note that the SLK230 was at the end of its production run in the US actually cheaper than at its launch. In 1997 it cost some $40,300. In 2003, the face-lifted model was sold at $40,265.

The SLK32 AMG

There are plenty of discussions on the internet about what constitutes an AMG model. Daimler AG sold and sells AMG Sport Packages or body kits for almost all of their models. This makes it difficult for many to distinguish between a real AMG and an AMG look-alike. Also on the second hand market, cars with the Sport Package are sometimes advertised as Mercedes AMG cars. But true AMG cars are distinguished by what is under the hood.

All AMG power plants (except R129 versions) have a silver engine cover, and from the third quarter of 2001 when the SL55 AMG R230 was introduced, these have also had the name of the technician who built that very engine, proudly displayed on a plaque atop of the engine cover – with an exception: this practice did not commence for the SLK32 until the introduction of the 2003 model.

By the way, AMG was not the first manufacturer to have started such a practice. That honor must go to Aston Martin, which had used it since the 1950s. It is a practice that can come quite handy, as a friend of the author found out in the 1970s. He had a problem with his AM engine and could not get the needed spare at any AM dealership (Google having not been invented yet).

So one day, out of desperation, he took his wife's Ford station wagon and drove up to AM headquarters, where he managed to sneak into the plant without anyone noticing. Knowing the mechanic's name from the plaque on the engine, he sure found after a bit of asking the man, who had built his car's power plant. After a fairly lengthy begging from my friend, the mechanic finally relented and took out that very spare from an engine, he was just building and gave it to him. According to my friend, all of this went on with no one looking and on top, no money had changed hands. The mechanic just handed the part to him and asked him to leave soonest.

A 2002 SL55 AMG V8 engine with the mechanic's plaque

Giorgio De Giuseppe had built this particular engine

Back from AM to AMG. AMG was founded by Hans Werner ***A***ufrecht and Erhard ***M***elcher in June 1967 as a racing shop. As with many other companies, the first two characters were borrowed from the last names of the two founders. The third character “G” in the AMG name did not come from the company’s first location, but from Aufrecht’s place of birth “***G***roßaspach”. Both gentlemen were former Daimler-Benz technicians, who initially offered engine performance packages and various unofficial upgrades and accessory packages for Daimler-Benz cars. Daimler-Benz engineers used to laugh at them due to their tiny business size.

They also did not take them too seriously because of their continuous underfunding problems. But over the years AMG managed to mature into a full-fledged racing company with its first major rally success in 1971. There they managed to score first in class and second overall behind a Ford Capri at the 24 hours race at Spa with their impressive 300SEL 6.3, called “Red Sow”. The 6.3 was actually a 6.8 and the story of this race with the preparation of it is alone worth a book. In 1990 AMG signed with Daimler-Benz a cooperation agreement and in January 1999, Daimler-Benz acquired 51 percent of the company. At that time the name was changed into Mercedes-AMG GmbH (Ltd.). AMG subsequently became a wholly owned subsidiary of Daimler AG, as of January 2005.

The first official model developed by AMG in 1991 was the AMG 500SL 6.0 V8 (M 119) R129 with Bosch KE injection, 374 hp at 5.500 rpm and a maximum torque of 550 Nm (405.7 ft-lbs) at 4.000 rpm.

Erhard Melcher in the very early AMG days

The question whether an AMG package for the SLK was really needed is rather academic. It was offered in most other Mercedes models, so it was only natural to have it in the little sports car too.

Maybe AMG additions to the Daimler-Benz line of cars were built with the famous adage of Adlai Stevenson in mind: *"Power corrupts, but lack of power corrupts absolutely"*. But to come back to the question of whether such a car was really needed, former head of AMG sales & marketing Mario Spitzner had this to say: "Naturally nobody does really need it, but on the other hand there is also no harm in owning it and to have plenty of fun with it. Our clients usually have more than one car. Many even own on top of the AMG car a Porsche or Ferrari".

First presented in autumn 2000, the SLK32 AMG (internal code: 170.466) became available in January 2001. Pre-production had already started in August 2000. When looking at the car, it did not reveal what explosive power the driver could expect.

AMG Sport Packages with fancy wheels were already available for some time on the "lesser" SLK models. Only the decision by Daimler-Benz to plant the 3.2 L V6 into the engine bay made it possible for the AMG technicians to work their magic on the SLK. It was the first time that AMG performed their tuning activities on a six-cylinder engine - all previous engines had been V8 power plants. The same engine was also utilized in the C32 AMG.

AMG had tried already in 1997 to put a longer 3.6 L straight six under the SLK's hood. But as they could not move the engine far enough back for proper weight distribution, they ended up with a bump on front of the hood. This was of course rejected by Daimler-Benz, however the honor of being the first company to cram a bigger engine into the car went to a tuner.

354 hp, 450 NM (331.9 ft-lbs) and a curb weight of just 1.5 tons could tell even the innocent bystander what to expect from this mean little brute (M112 E32, internal code: 112.960). It flew from 0 to 100 km/h in just 5.2 seconds, offered fistfuls of low- and midrange torque, but had like all other AMG cars its top speed electronically governed at 250 km/h (155 mph).

With the limiter removed, it could achieve 291 km/h (181 mph). It could also finish the quarter mile in a mere 13.2 seconds at 177 km/h or 110 mph (SLK230: 15.6 s at 147.7 km/h or 91.8 mph). It offered the same peak horsepower as the E55 with a 5.5 L V8. Finally, Daimler-Benz had a car that could rival the BMW M Roadster and Porsche Boxster S.

After the successful launch of the SL55 AMG, the SLK was finally also "AMG-ed"

This most exciting SLK engine version to date, was fitted with a belt-driven Lysholm-type helical twin-screw compressor, twirling at 20,650 rpm and cramming about 44 pounds of intercooled air per minute into the car's cylinders at two times atmospheric pressure. A water-to-air intercooler, which sat between the cylinder banks with the compressor, was connected to a separate front-mounted radiator and was responsible for cooling the intake charge. That way more power could be generated, while the risk of pre-ignition was minimized. This compressor, more efficient than a Roots-type design, was developed in conjunction with the Japanese industrial giant Ishikawajima-Harima Industries IHI and offered Teflon-coated rotors, which produced an overall boost of 14.5 psi. Its 354 hp became available at 6,100 rpm, while its maximum torque was delivered between 3,000 and 4,600 rpm. Ninety percent of it was already available at 2,300 rpm. In order to save fuel and assist in emission compliance, the compressor was designed to stay dormant via an electronic coupling during normal driving conditions until the engine speed reached 2,900 rpm. However, should the driver hit the floor like an excited teenager, it would engage instantaneously and the car would burst off the line with plenty of rear tire smoke. Switch off ESP and it will give you even more smoke.

Red was not as popular with SLK32 owners, most were bought in silver and black

However, it was not only the compressor that was added to the V6. Other components of the engine had to be replaced with stronger alternatives in order to make the power plant as bulletproof as its more docile origin. These included a new crankshaft, upgraded camshafts, connecting rods and pistons. In addition, a revised oil pump and new valve springs were added. Bore and stroke were left unchanged at 89.9x84.0 mm, while the compression ratio was reduced from 10.0 to 9.0:1. The car was offered only with the newly developed AMG five-gear speed-shift automatic (W5 A 580). Daimler-Benz just did not have a manual transmission that was capable of handling all the torque. AMG claimed that it could execute gear shifts some 35 percent faster than the standard SLK gearbox. And it also chose, when accelerating, the most appropriate gear to bring all that power on the tarmac.

In fast corners, it managed to stay in the chosen gear in order to avoid unwanted load change reactions, something the standard SLK auto box in the earlier cars was not really famous for. Even better, when the driver touched the brake pedal, it shifted down as to mimic a manual shifter. The transmission came also with lower (numerically speaking) transmission gears and a rear axle ratio of 3.07:1. Like on the other SLKs it came with the *TouchShift* manual gear-shifting capability. But the transmission had such a useful shifting program that shifting manually was not really a necessity.

A small spoiler lip with integrated brake light at the trailing edge of the trunk lid reduced the rear airlift at higher speeds by fifty percent

Car and Driver tested the car in 2001 and had this to say about the transmission: *The SportShift tranny is admittedly well mated to the engine. Its torque converter locks up in every gear but first and reverse for efficiency, and the shifts are 35 percent quicker than in lesser SLK slush boxes. It also downshifts under braking and does an admirable job of gear selection. But like a headstrong teenager, it resists manual control, overriding the driver with its own up- and downshifts. Bottom line: We'd prefer the six-speed stick found in other SLKs.*

Although the car came with the same 17 in tire sizes as an SLK fitted with AMG Sport Package, it came with great looking unique twin five-spoke alloy wheels. Tires came either from Michelin or Pirelli. In order to accommodate the power, the suspension had been reinforced with stiffer shocks and springs, which were also shorter, so that the body could be lowered by some 2.5 cm (1.0 in).

The brakes came with vented discs front and rear, which were further enlarged to 332 mm (13.0 in) at the front and 300 mm (11.8 in) at the rear. They also had bigger calipers and rotors. Naturally the car came with an AMG specific high-flow, low-back-pressure exhaust with twin chrome exhaust tips. It excited the enthusiast with a quiet, yet growling and deep-chested masculine sound. What a welcome change to what the four-cylinder cars had to offer in this department.

Twin five-spoke alloys were unique to the SLK32

The AMG apron was already known from the sport package

The Sport Package optional on other SLKs was standard for the SLK32. Its improved air -dams were intended to help balance aerodynamic lift front-to-rear and enable an higher top speed. The lower air intake had been enlarged and gave the car with its mesh insert a more dynamic appearance. Unfortunately, the grille did not offer a matching mesh. Both front fenders featured a V6 Kompressor badge. A small spoiler lip with integrated brake light at the trailing edge of the trunk lid reduced aerodynamic lift at the rear at higher speeds by up to fifty percent. Weighing in at 1.495 kg, the car was some 90 kg heavier than its more civilized cousin. AMG stated that it had a production capacity of some 2,000 engines for the SLK32 annually.

Inside, the car offered more strongly-bolstered, heated seats with special two-tone grey Nappa leather, silver-grey stitching and AMG emblems pressed into the integrated headrests. Other seat colors were of course available too. The machined aluminum trim was replaced by dark birds-eye maple wood and the instruments had a silver fascia with AMG emblem and speed markings up to 300 km/h (in the US: 180 mph). Also the steering wheel was AMG-specific.

What it lacked though, despite its price tag, was a CD player. A CD changer for the trunk was even here an optional extra. One could either opt for the K2 Package (option code 177) for $1,795 or the K2a Package with voice activation (option code 179). Both came with a Motorola Startac cellular phone. A CD changer without the phone was never officially offered by Daimler-Benz. One had to go to a DB dealer or another trusted audio-retailer source instead.

Seats were heated and had integrated headrests with AMG logo

European speedos were calibrated up to 300 km/h,

Prices for the SLK32 started in the UK at £44,500, while in the US it cost $55,500 and in Germany €56,000. That made it some $10,000 more expensive than an equally powerful BMW M Roadster. There were three things though that the BMW lacked, the build quality of the Benz, the vario-roof and the option to have an automatic transmission, as the BMW came "only" with a manual one. As already mentioned earlier, in case the potential SLK32 owner wanted his new toy with manual transmission, he was out of luck.

A nice greeting, when the passengers entered the SLK32

The special editions

Special editions are offered to keep interest high in some automotive models. This practice has been known and widely used by many manufacturers for decades. Not so for Daimler-Benz; they only started to take note of such a marketing ploy with the R129 SL in 1994, when they looked for ways to stimulate interest in the big roadster. It obviously worked to their satisfaction: from 1994 through to the end of the production of that series in 2001, they offered it in more than 15 special editions.

In 1997 it became the SLK's turn. In this case there was no need really to help push the cars out of the showrooms. The SLK had just been launched, and sold beyond anyone's expectation. DB did offer in those early years a few attractive low-volume editions, which complimented the bigger SL special editions. Its first such model was a "Mille Miglia" edition, limited to just 40 units, of which 15 were reserved for Germany. Daimler-Benz had brought out in 1995 its first Mille Miglia edition of the R129 SL in order to commemorate the 40th anniversary of Stirling Moss' and Denis Jenkinson's win of the road race in the 300SLR #722. Of that SL500 just 10 were produced.

Just for comparison purpose, this is the 1995 SL Mille Miglia version

The SLK ***"Mille Miglia"*** version was limited to the SLK230 and finished in brilliant silver with a Mille Miglia sticker attached to the right side of the trunk lid. It also had somewhat unusual looking three-spoke 16 in alloy wheels and blue-illuminated scuff plates with Mille Miglia logo. Inside the car, there was leather upholstery in Scarlet red that also covered the center console and part of the steering wheel. The roof lining and floor mats were in black, the latter also had red piping and special Mille Miglia embroidery.

Unique Mille Miglia three-spoke alloys did not really make the car more attractive

Red leather not only covered portions of the seats and steering wheel, but also the center console around the gearshift

A second special edition, called ***"Limited Edition"*** was offered from December 1999 onwards. Painted in Obsidian Black metallic, it came with polished aluminum six-spoke 7.5J x 17" ET37 EVO II alloys and a polished stainless steel exhaust tip. Inside it offered a two-tone Charcoal-Oyster interior with matching gear shift knob plus a Package K2 CD-changer with Digital Cellular Phone. Limited Edition badges were affixed to the floor mats, key chain and trunk lid.

The third and fourth special editions were offered starting April/May 2002 towards the end of the SLK R170 life. The third edition was again a ***"Mille Miglia"*** version, offered only for the SLK320. Just twelve units, which were partly produced with some of the tools of the original 190SL, were to be sold. The car was painted in Silver Arrow metallic, but other colors were also possible.

The leather was colored in Designo classic red with the steering wheel offering a leather/wood combination. Dark birds-eye maple wood was fitted instead of aluminum trim. The black velour floor mats had red piping and the Mille Miglia logo embroidered.

The instruments featured a rather unusual touch, as their fascia was styled in a classic 190SL design. The doorsills had illuminated scuff plates made of stainless steel with “SLK Mille Miglia Edition 2002” on it. The front grille had a nice-looking polished aluminum-mesh look, while the front fenders featured a SLK Mille Miglia Edition 2002 badge on both sides. AMG Styling III wheels in 7,5J x 17" with 225/45 front and 8,5J x 17" with 245/40 rear tires completed the package.

The instruments had a vintage 190SL look

The fourth version, called ***"Special Edition"*** was limited to 2,000 units. It featured seven-spoke 7.5J x 17" ET37 alloy wheels and SLK - Special Edition badges on both side of the front fenders. Inside, the car offered heated and perforated black Nappa leather seats with contrasting machined aluminum trim on the center console and around the door handles. Black leather also covered the rollover bars, the airbag area and the gearshift knob, which had its top covered with a chrome badge with "SLK - Special Edition" lettering. The aluminum gearshift console was surrounded by a chrome frame.

Special carpets had silver-grey piping, while the instruments came with a silver fascia, white pointers with silver cap and orange instead of black lettering. The car was painted in Brilliant Silver, had the six-speed manual transmission and was available for all models except the SLK32. Other colors were available also.

Twin seven-spoke alloys were similar in design to the five-spoke AMG rims

The elegant looking aluminum-grille was not used for the lower air intake

Initially the cars had perforated leather seats

2004 Special Edition cars appear to have the Final Edition version seats without perforation

The fifth and last edition series became available in May 2003, called ***“Final Edition”.*** How many were produced is unfortunately not known, but it can be assumed that it was no more than 2,000 units. On the outside, it had the polished aluminum mesh-look grille with SLK - Final Edition badges on the sides of both front fenders. The vario-roof and A-pillar had polished aluminum lids around the edges and elegant-looking ten-spoke alloy wheels in “Alcyone”-design in 7J x 16" with 205/55 tires front and 8J x 16" with 225/50 tires rear. Optionally “Icenio Saidak” or AMG wheels could be ordered with 7,5J x 17" alloys and 225/45 tires on the front set and 8,5J x 17" with 245/40 on the rear set of rims.

This car came fitted with the AMG alloys

A striking red interior might not be to everyone's liking, but it is a fine match to the Brilliant Silver paint

This Final Edition model could be ordered in five exterior paint schemes. Inside, the car offered the same features as the "Special Edition", but was also available in Classic Red. The leather seats were not perforated this time. Except for the V6 version, the cars were not available with air-conditioning in most European markets. The machined aluminum trim could be exchanged for dark birds-eye maple. As with the "Special Edition", it was available for all three SLK models except the SLK32.

This last edition should be seen as the last hurrah for a vehicle that had aged very gracefully and was soon to be replaced by a more modern successor. It was consequently advertised in the SLK sales brochure over three full pages with glowing words:

The 2004 SLK Special Editions offer up a true challenge. Should you stop to admire the sunlight glint of 17" twin-spoke alloy wheels, the silver painted grille and the subtle rear spoiler, perhaps running your fingers across the special badges and contemplating the compelling value contained within such a beauty?

Or is it better to turn those wheels into a blur and enjoy the SLK230 Kompressor's instantaneous 192 supercharged horse-power or the relentless urge of the SLK320's V-6? Or maybe you should just bask in the Charcoal Nappa Leather upholstery—it even covers the roll bars—and consider, which of the five available exterior colors really suits you. The choice is yours. The result is always the same—pure exhilaration."

And it continues:

The SLK Special Editions have a profound effect wherever they go. The wind is tamed by a subtle rear spoiler. Corners are straightened by 17" twin-spoke alloy wheels wearing 225/45ZR 17 front and 245/40ZR 17 rear high-performance tires. And the eyes of passerby are delighted by special chrome badges, just as their hearts are tossed toward desire.

Alternative black interior

The sales performance

That sales of the R170 turned out to be a positive surprise for Daimler-Benz is a slight understatement. The car was an instant hit, and management had serious problems initially to cope with demand. Production capacity at the Bremen plant, which also produced the SL, was set-up at 32,000 units annually, but after just a few months, 55,000 units had been sold and the old Mercedes disease hit again: a waiting list of up to 24 months. At such a large plant as Bremen, capacity cannot be increased overnight, so the workforce had to work extended shifts on six days a week.

This eventually caused friction with unions and resulted in strikes, which worsened the capacity problems and extended the waiting time even further. People in Europe were so eager to get hold of an SLK that prices of up to DM 15,000 over the suggested retail price of DM 60,950 for a SLK230 were asked and paid. Luckily for the SLK fans, production issues were finally fixed in 1997, so that in that year 48,000 units rolled off the assembly line. As might be expected, the most popular model proved to be the SLK230, of which some 113,520 units sold from July 1996 to February 2000, 85,321 of these were fitted with automatic transmission. The SLK's largest market was North America and its popularity did not decrease over time, as Mercedes sold consistently well-over 30,000 units annually. This would change with the face-lifted model, which had its best year in 2000 when it found 15,860 buyers. By 2003, those numbers had decreased to 7,260 units. All told, sales of the pre- and post-facelift SLK230s amounted to 160,825 units, accounting for more than half of the total R170 production. Of the 47,305 face-lifted cars, 36,987 were bought with automatic transmission.

The second most popular model was the face-lifted SLK200 Kompressor, produced from February 2000 until April 2004. It managed to attract 55,449 buyers, of which 21,878 chose an automatic transmission. This clearly demonstrates that European customers preferred the manual car.

It was similar with the pre-facelift SLK200, where just 13,928 automatic cars out of a total of 44,846 cars were sold. The smallest SLK had its best year in 2001, when 16,550 units were sold. By 2003, sales had dropped to 9,811 units. The SLK200 Kompressor, which was sold in some southern European markets until early 2000, was never offered with an automatic transmission. Of that car 12,353 units were produced.

Naturally, the SLK320 had the highest share of automatic transmissions with 28,854 units out of 33,416 produced. The model with the lowest overall sales was of course the SLK32 AMG. AMG had a production capacity of 2,000 engines annually. From January 2001 till March 2004 a total of 4,333 of this variant were produced, with production peaking in 2001 with 2,193 units sold. In its last full production year, 2003, a total of 742 cars found a buyer. Of all SLK32 AMGs produced, the majority of 2,056 were sold into the US, 979 units were sold in Germany, and 263 units found a home in the UK (some sources say 271 units). The cheaper BMW M-Roadster performed a bit better, as it sold in the last three full production years 7,401 units.

In total 311,222 SLK R170s were produced, out of which 119,921 were ordered with manual and 191,301 with automatic transmission. The first SLK had managed to establish a market segment that grew exponentially over the years. It also managed to capture the largest share of that market and it remained popular throughout its production run.

Although it has to be said that due to more competitors fielding entrants within the same niche, sales went downhill from 2001 onwards. While in all previous years, total sales hovered around 50,000 units annually, they decreased in 2001 to 42,182. They took a steep decline the following year to just 28,244 units, which was followed in 2002 by a mere 21,190 units. It was time for a change.

A substantial number of the car's elements lived on until 2008 in the Chrysler Crossfire. As for the aforementioned Z3, BMW produced some 279,273 of these vehicles from 1995 to 2002, while Porsche managed to sell 160,000 Boxsters from 1996 to 2004. In comparison, the car that had started the small roadster revolution, the Mazda MX5/Miata, sold in its first generation from 1990 to 1998 close to 500,000 units.

One year later, the Miata hit the Guinness Book of World Records, where it was declared the best-selling two-seat sports car in history with a total production of 531,890 units. Given the fact that the Mazda was much cheaper, the sales performance of the R170 can only be judged as excellent. A detailed sales breakdown can be found at the end of this book.

Experiencing the SLK230 Kompressor

Looking at the car from a distance, it looks cute. This is probably not, what Daimler-Benz or for that matter most owners might want to hear, but it is still better than remarks from automotive journalists, who referred to it occasionally as the "hairdresser's car". I have never seen a car specifically designed for hairdressers, but this is not it. It would also be a bit unfair to Michael Maurer, who did a great job designing the first generation SLK and who does a superb job now looking after the modern Porsche designs.

But let us not waste our time looking at the car, let us drive it. For someone like me, who is 6.3 ft tall, getting into the SLK230 is a bit of a squeeze. But once settled in the driver's seat, everything is fine, a bit tight, but ok. Looking around in the closed car, I can understand why people like the car over the BMW and Porsche competition, as it offers more security and a quieter ride than its ragtop roofed German siblings. But with the top up, it joins them with fairly big rear blind spots. On the other hand, as a typical Mercedes it impresses top down with its structural integrity and no flexing or creaking even on less than perfect roads.

Switching on the engine does not excite that much, as the sound is too ordinary for such a car. No wonder, Daimler-Benz offered special AMG-style mufflers to help compensate for this. But that is enough complaining, because the fun part starts right now: the car does not only offer a fairly spirited acceleration, thanks to the double-wishbone axle at front and the five-link suspension at the rear, it also rushes through the slalom cones at 107.8 km/h (67.3 mph).

Mind you that is even more impressive than a contemporary Chevrolet Corvette C5. It runs the quarter mile in 15.2 seconds at 147.7 km/h (91.8 mph). It also circles the skid pad pulling 0.89 g and is capable of stopping from 100 km in a scant 35.3 m (116 ft). In case you have forgotten, we talk here about a smallish 2.3 l four-cylinder car.

Although it does not come with the turbo lag that can be found with turbocharged engines at lower revs, the compressor or supercharger really does not come to life until the rev counter hits around 3,000 rpm, with the excitement hitting the red line at 5,800 rpm.

The manual shift adds considerably to the fun factor

The suspension instills confidence and almost begs you for deep corner dives. This feels simply fantastic. “Come on, throw me around and keep that broad grin on your face”, the car seems to encourage me. If you expect the car to be choppy or sports car rough, you will be in for a pleasant dis-appointment, as the suspension and the spring-loaded seats absorb much of the roughness coming through from the street's surface. The SLK230 acts like a true roadster, while offering its passengers an almost eerily pleasant ride over just about any rotten pavement.

The excitement increases even further if the car is fitted with the manual transmission, because the change is not just of mechanical nature, suddenly there is a completely different car and driver interaction possible. No review in a magazine or video on *YouTube* can describe the feeling you get with the action of this five-speed box. Ok, it is not as precise as the one in the first Porsche Boxster, and some even mentioned that it was a bit rubbery. And while we are at it, yes, the steering feels a bit wobbly too.

But there are compensations! It is such an absolute blast to wind up the ever eager engine in each gear by hand, feel the supercharger come in with its special whirring sound and above all have no electronic rev-limiter kick you out of excitement at 5,800 rpm (it does that at 6,200 rpm though). Now, that's what driving is all about. With this SLK Daimler-Benz had really re-invented itself. Of course the later introduced (better sounding) six-cylinder and especially the AMG version could do all this and then much more. But in all honesty, this Kompressor engine with its 192 hp is all, a normal human being really needs in a light two-seater sports car. Especially, when the engine is mated to the manual transmission. When the hardtop is up, the car is almost sedan-quiet, which can be attributed not only to its perfect fit but also to the fully padded headliner. For most owners the SLK proves to be the best of both worlds, as it is able to accommodate your changing moods as easily as the changing weather. The small 2.3 l is almost as fast as the more expensive and thirstier SLK320, although I have to admit its lacks a bit that car's effortless power output. But this is natural, given the six-cylinder's larger displacement. All in all, the car is just fantastic and one of the best remedies against street boredom. At the time of its launch in 1996, this SLK was for its price and fun factor the best car Daimler-Benz had to offer. Period.

And yes, I am aware what Jeremy Clarkson once said about the SLK230: "this miserable 2.3 liter engine belongs in a kitchen utensil, not a sports car". Well, it will most certainly not end up in my kitchen.

The Brabus SLK6.5-32

Any Mercedes car is nowadays a subject for tuning. Even a stately Maybach, although no longer produced, is and has been heavily altered. So it should be no wonder that the SLK was especially embraced by the tuning scene, when it was launched in 1996. You may ask yourself, why on earth does anyone in his right mind want a car that has even more horsepower than the "standard" SLK32 AMG. After all the AMG throws already 354 hp at a curb weight of just 1.5 tons. Well, it's all a question of perception. Once you have driven the little AMG brute for a few weeks, you might ask yourself indeed, whether there isn't anything faster available. Just for the pure fun of it of course.

The most popular tuner in Germany for anything Mercedes, next to AMG of course, is Brabus. And after AMG had been finally swallowed by Daimler-Chrysler in 1999, Brabus remains one of only two independent large European tuners (the other one is Carlsson) that concentrates solely on Mercedes cars. Founded in 1977 by Klaus **Bra**ckmann and Bodo **Bus**chmann, this fully-recognized automotive manufacturer nowadays sells around 8,000 cars per annum. It was rumored at the end of the 1990s that at least five Daimler-Benz executive board members had their AMG based company cars further tuned by Brabus.

Humble beginnings: Brabus in its early days

One of the first SLK cars offered by **Brabus** soon after the launch of the R170 was the SLK6.5-32, or Type R170E65, as it was called by Brabus. Its engine was based on the M119 500SL V8, first launched in 1990 in a slightly milder version as R129 SL6.0-32. This 6.0 offered 408 hp with an impressive torque of 560 NM (413 lbs-ft), available at 3,800 rpm. Seven years later, Brabus' chief tech-honcho and former Daimler-Benz engineer Ulrich Gauffrés felt that he could do better. Brabus owner Bodo Buschmann calls him respectfully "the professor". The problem was that Daimler-Benz would stop producing the famous four-valves-per-cylinder M119 in 1998 in exchange for the three valves-per-cylinder M113. The older (and better) DOHC engine with Bosch KE-Jetronic was based on the 1980 M117 and showed up in such fantastic cars as the 500SL R107. It had seen an upgrade in autumn 1992 to a so-called standard deck design with Bosch LH-Jetronic, which made it useable in its basic set-up for all Mercedes V8 applications at that time.

Nothing on the outside tells about the car's fierce potential

Brabus is established in Germany as automotive manufacturer

The new 1998 modular SOHC M 113 V8 had less metal available to increase the bore as needed. This limited its ultimate capacity to 6.1 liters and so far Brabus had only managed to squeeze 420 hp out of it. So in an arrangement with Daimler-Benz, Brabus would receive for the next few years fifty of the old pre-1992 closed deck M 119 engine-blocks annually for its tuning activities.

The 1997 Brabus SLK had the previous 6.0 L design enlarged to 6.5 L. The near square bore and stroke of 101 x 100 mm was made possible with a new long-throw crank. It was machined from a steel billet married to new lightweight alloy pistons and lightened and carefully balanced standard rods. Other goodies included a polished intake manifold, high lift cams, free-flow air-cleaners, gas-flowed heads and sports metal catalysts. The standard injectors could stay in place, though the modified ECU informed them to stay open for longer. A new ignition curve was burned into the electronic chip and then it was time to test the new masterpiece's mettle.

Mr. Gauffrés must have been pleased, when the data records showed that the engine offered 450 hp at 5,900 rpm with an even more impressive torque of 662 NM (488.3 ft-lbs) at 3,800 rpm. Eighty percent of that torque was already available at 1,000 rpm. The standard AMG five-speed electronically controlled speed-shift automatic trans-mission was beefy enough for the engine and could be used without further strengthening.

Naturally, it was not only the engine that received an upgrading. With all that power available, many of the components aft of the transmission (which, by the way, came from the contemporary S-class), needed to be tinkered with. The propeller shaft and rear differential were both bespoke items. All the anchor points of the rear axle with the suspension were strengthened. The differential was replaced with one from the S-class, but with special internals and a strengthened rear axle plate. The steel half plates, located on each side of the differential, were reinforced and welded together to form a cage.

Although the V8 was actually not much heavier (and not much bigger) than the 2.3 L four-cylinder with its iron block, Brabus did strengthen the engine's cross member and its anchor points to the body-shell. Most of the weight increase in the engine bay came from increased oil coolers for engine and gearbox plus a larger radiator. The suspension offered stiffer springs and dampers, a larger anti-roll bar at the front and a new one at the rear. In addition, the Alcon brakes were enlarged to 330 mm (13.0 in) and four calipers at front and 300 mm (11.8 in) with two calipers at the rear. The car rode on Brabus Monoblock IV three-piece alloy wheels with 225/40 ZR18 on 8.5J x 18" at the front and 255/35 ZR18 on 9.5J x 18" at the rear.

450 hp with 660 MN is quite a statement in this relatively small car

They filled out the wheel arches quite nicely. With a full tank and no passengers, the Brabus SLK had a curb weight of 1,520 kg (3,344 lbs), which was, despite all the stiffening and strengthening, just 25 kg (55 lbs) greater than that of the SLK32 AMG, and was distributed 53/47 percent front to rear.

The brutal punch of the V8 was a revelation, as was its sound, a deep burbling growl, quite the feast for the ears. It stormed within 4.5 seconds from 0 to 100 km/h and achieved, if electronically ungoverned, a top speed of 302 km/h (187 mph). With the speed limiter in place, its top speed was set at 285 km/h (177 mph). Just 16 seconds were needed to reach 200 km/h (124 mph). All that force that the driver had to use the accelerator pedal with great caution and finesse, because otherwise it would just result in rear tire rubber being converted to smoke, even at speeds exceeding 100 km/h.

Next to the engine, also the bespoke interior was nothing short of sensational with its Bugatti- blue mastik-leather color and special stitching. It came with a lovely custom birds-eye maple wood with aluminum gearshift and handbrake lever. Naturally, any other color could be ordered too.

Some of the SLKs came with a light yellow interior called "Sunshine", which offered a nice contrast to a black exterior. If all that was not impressive enough, you had not asked for the price yet. Or as the old saying goes, if you had to, you could not afford the car. Bodo Buschmann once said that one SLK kilometer at Brabus cost DM100.-. He did not elaborate, whether he meant the real or electronically limited top speed. But as the car was priced at DM 313,200 incl. VAT ($176,900, or £110,900 at 1997 exchange rates), it was fairly obvious, what he had meant. This also ensured that such a car would only sell in tiny, homoeopathic numbers. His clientele would certainly not mind, not seeing another Brabus SLK in their home town. A total number of 14 SLK65-32 were built, two of them RHD.

The author never had the luck to experience such marvel, but a certain Jeremy Clarkson of BBC Top Gear fame did in 1997 and 2000. In his first test in 1997 he was most impressed with the car's sheer, unadulterated power and the superb handling for such a short-wheel-based car. He declared the car "perfect", and remarked that it showed a performance that was better than that of an Aston Martin Vantage. In 2000, he ranked it the best overall sports car - on top of all others. That was before he treated himself to an SL55 AMG R230. But that is for another story.

An interior option was luxurious "Mastik" leather

It was an expensive feast not only for the eyes, but also the nose

Brabus used its own fascia

Brabus of course had also less powerful options for the R170 available. For the SLK230, they offered various engine kits, which increased power from 210 hp to 250 hp. The SLK320 kit could be bought with either 233 hp or 243 hp, while the SLK32 kit offered also a less powerful version with "only" 378 hp at $8,050.

Other tuners

Väth should find a mention here, because they were actually the first tuner, who managed in 1996 to fit a 3.5 L straight-six into the new car's engine bay. They succeeded by fabricating and installing adapter plates, which helped to move the longer engine a bit further aft, so that no bump at the front was needed. This had the additional benefit of bettering the weight distribution.

They used as a basis the Mercedes M 104 3.2 L engine, already available for several Mercedes models since 1992 and named their car *"SLK V35"*. First they increased the bore, installed special pistons to increase compression; then they polished the cylinder heads and installed bigger valves plus special valve springs. After fine tuning the ECU and changing the camshaft, the displacement had grown to 3,452 cc (210.7 cu in) and the power output rose from 213 hp to 286 hp. The torque had grown to 390 NM (287.6 ft-lbs) and the top speed was a respectable 270 km/h (167.7 mph).

Väth was the first tuner to install a larger engine in the SLK

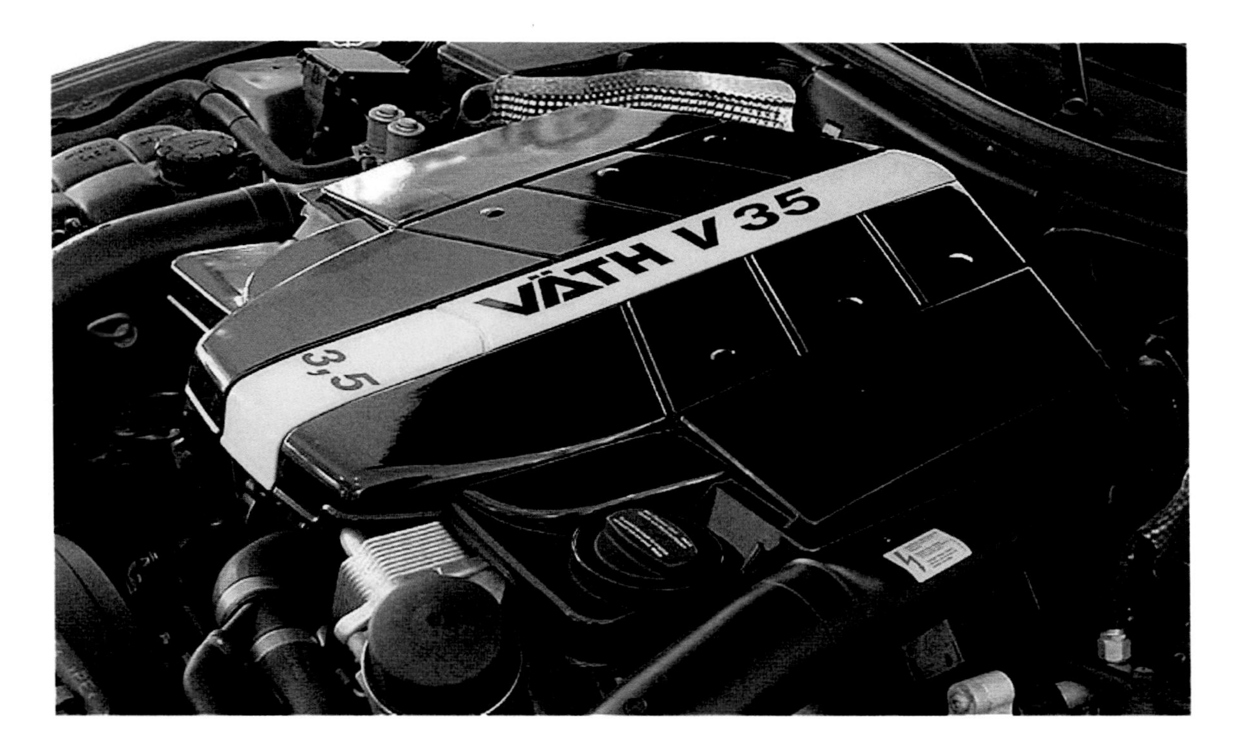

Later Väth offers included a performance package for the SLK32, which boosted the power to 395 hp and a maximum torque of 510 NM (376.2 ft-lbs) at 4,400 rpm, which guaranteed a top speed of 282 km/h (175.2 mph). Although the car offered considerably less power than the Brabus, its top speed was just 3 km/h shy of the Brabus'.

***Carlsson*,** who concentrate like Brabus solely on Daimler AG cars, was founded by brothers Andreas and Rolf Hartge in 1989. Although based in Germany, it was named after Swedish rally icon Ingvar Carlsson, who served in the early years as the company's technical partner.

For the R170, Carlsson offered four tuning kits from 204 hp (a kit called CK20, for the SLK200 Kompressor) to 245 hp (kit name: CK32, for the SLK320). The two CK23 kits offered 225 hp for the pre-facelift and 230 hp for the face-lifted version. Although the power increase was somewhat modest, it was its availability through a wide rpm band that impressed most. Prices ranged from €2,125 (CK20) to €3,642 (CK23 pre-facelift), €2,357 (CK23 face-lifted) and €4,986 (CK32). These prices did not include an upgraded exhaust system, wider rims or an adapted suspension. The suspension package offered stiffer Carlsson springs and shocks for €1,750.

The big Carlsson alloys are a tight fit for the wheel arches

The best-known Mercedes tuner in the US is **RENNtech**, which was founded in 1989 by Hartmut Feyhl. Before forming RENNtech, Hartmut had worked with AMG, had become their technical director in the US and was largely responsible for the amazing AMG Hammer, based on the W124 E-class cars. Today RENNtech does not concentrate only on Mercedes cars, but has specialized on several European automotive brands, among them Ferrari, Audi, Porsche and BMW.

RENNtech offered for the SLK various "Performance Packages". They started with the SLK230, where a larger crankshaft pulley, priced at $1,195, was responsible for a power gain of 20 hp to 212 hp and an increase in torque of some ten percent to 300 NM (221 ft-lbs).

Three packages were available for the SLK320. The lowest was an ECU upgrade, which increased the power output from 218 to 225 hp at a cost of $1,295. A modest torque increase of 16 NM (12 ft-lbs) to 330 (243 ft-lbs) came with it. For $9,995 one could ask for something more substantial.

A RENNtech optimized ECU

The engine was enlarged to 3.8 L and its power boosted to 262 hp, while torque saw an increase of 90 NM (66 ft-lbs) to an impressive 400 NM (295 ft-lbs). If that was not enough, a further $5,000 added new camshafts and ported/polished cylinder heads to the package.

That way, the SLK320 offered 291 hp and a maximum torque of 298 NM (302 ft-lbs), which were available from 3,800 to 5,000 rpm. All other packages had no change in their rpm band from the standard cars.

RENNtech offered also for the SLK32 AMG three packages, starting again with an ECU upgrade for $1,995, which increased power by 25 to 374 hp. Torque gained 27 NM (20 ft-lbs) to a total of 480 NM (354 ft-lbs), available from 2,700 to 5,000 rpm (standard AMG: 3,000 to 4,600 rpm). For $3,495 the customer received next to the ECU upgrade a larger crankshaft pulley and an increase of 45 to 394 hp. Torque was lifted by 80 NM (60.5 ft-lbs) to 530 NM (391 ft-lbs) available already from 2,700 to 5,000 rpm. An additional $11,500 enabled the car to hit Brabus territory at a bargain. The enlarged 3.8 L six-cylinder engine offered 450 hp at 5,600 rpm and delivered a maximum torque of 590 NM (435 ft-lbs) from 3,200 to 5,200 rpm. Very, very impressive.

Of course, tuning did not stop there. Now you had the power, but you still lacked the looks. A decent set of 18 x 8.5" (9.5" at the rear) ten-spoke Monolites set you back another $4,700, while a rear sub-frame modification cost another $2,300. In order to get the best possible sound, a cat-back exhaust with resonator at $990 was of course a must!

Without going overboard, the following two photos are just samples from other German tuners. Like Brabus or RENNtech they concentrate on the technical side and offer various body kits. One of the next chapters is named: *Unique SLKs*. It shows a few examples of companies and individuals, who have tried to change the car into something completely different.

Lumma Tuning *resides in Winterlingen in southern Germany and offers for the R170 a quite aesthetic looking body kit for the R170*

Prior *is located in Kamp-Lintfort in the center of Germany and offers anything from engine tuning to body designs*

Choosing the right R170

The best advice is of course to have your used SLK inspected at an authorized dealer BEFORE any money changes hands. This will cost between $100 and $250 depending on the depth of inspection and will save you potentially not only a lot of frustration but more importantly also money. It is in general also advisable to buy a car with a properly documented service history.

The following list is by no means complete, but the author believes that it covers a reasonable share of issues that should be checked by a prospective buyer of the R170. Many of the points mentioned can be used for any car, but some are SLK specific. Quite a few of the potential problems can actually be fixed relatively easy, if one is a bit experienced. All points have been identified as either "*Easy To Fix*: **ETF**" or "*Dealer To Fix*: **DTF**".

It needs to be mentioned here that the author takes no responsibility for any outcome of this. The recommendations given here should serve as a guide. That is why no prices for spares or repairs are given, as this varies from country to country. As already stated in an earlier chapter, please do not expect this to be a manual for car maintenance or repairs, because that is not this book's purpose. There are much better publications available in that regard. As the SLK shares many parts with the W202 C-class, Haynes publication in the UK can be a good source, if technical issues need to be addressed.

Body:

1. Although the first SLK is well built and offers good resistance against corrosion, rust can be an issue in certain areas. Luckily most such occurrences are non-structural. Rust should be checked on the front fenders, the rear wheel arches, the hood slam panel and the area around the trunk lock (pre-facelift) and sometimes the trunk handle. If you find corrosion, give the car a very thorough in-spection, especially of the underside.

If the SLK in question is at a location, where it cannot be lifted up for inspection underneath, do yourself a favor and walk away, unless you are willing to accept certain risks and can get the car at a bargain.

It is difficult to say, whether early SLKs rust more often that late model versions, as it all depends on how the car has been treated. Naturally early SLKs are older, so in theory, there should be more rust on them, but in general early SLKs have the same rust prevention as newer models. **ETF**

2. Have a look inside the wheel-wells for loose or missing screws. **ETF**

3. Naturally you should have a look for any accident repair. One sign could be a poorly executed overspray. **ETF**

4. Ask, whether the car had an accident and if yes, was it repaired at an authorized service site such as the DB-dealer. Especially rear damage can be troublesome for the vario-roof, if not properly repaired. If in question, do walk away from that particular car, there are plenty others available. **DTF**

5. Open and close doors, trunk, hood and check for any leaks, worn out hinges, lack of support etc. **ETF**

6. Are all badges/emblems still in place. **ETF**

7. If the car has xenon headlights, are they original or after-market? When after-market, the washers and dynamic headlight leveling are most likely missing. Some cheap after-market xenon lights are prone to leaks. **ETF**

8. Check, whether trunk seals are good. If not, water can run into the pneumatic pump for central door locking, located under the jack in a foam jacket at the right side of the trunk. **ETF**

Wheels, brakes and exhaust:

1. Check tires for unusual or uneven wear. This may mean that front or rear wheels tracking is off, which can cause, if neglected over a long period of time, expensive repairs to either front or rear suspension. It can also be a sign that the previous owner had pushed the car frequently pretty hard or used it often on drives over roads with pot holes. **ETF**

2. Another sign of a previously hard life for the car can be unusual wear of brake rotors and/or brake pad linings. **DTF**

3. Do alloys have scratched rim edges? If yes, it is mostly a cosmetic issue. Question is, can you live with this or will you want to buy new ones? **ETF**

4. Check for worn-out ball joints, grab each tire with both hands and push from side to side (while tire is out of contact with the ground). They should not have any major movement. **DTF**

5. Is the spare still available with all its accessories such as the inflator. If there is no spare, is the TireFit kit still in the trunk. ETF

6. Drive the car on an empty road at a speed of 6-9 mpH / 10-15 km/h, then gently apply the brakes with your hands lightly on the steering wheel. The SLK should hold its course without moving to one side. If not, the brake pads need replacement in most cases. **ETF**

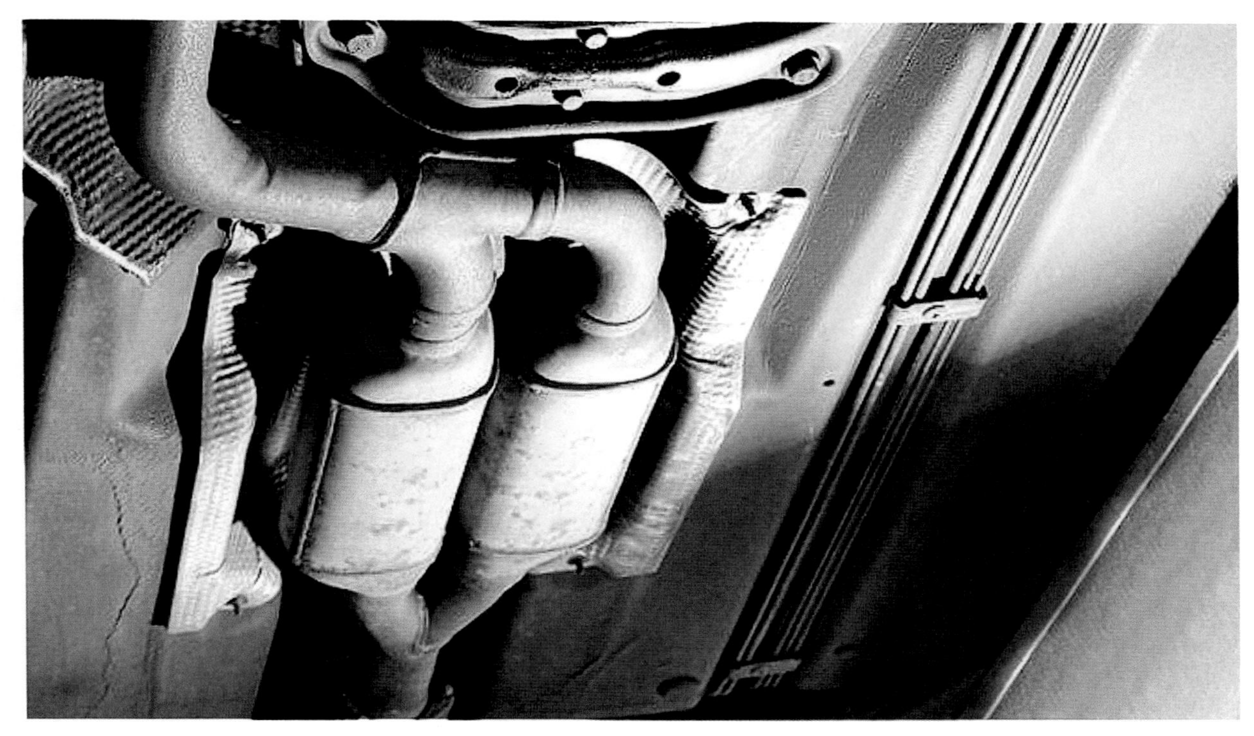

Catalytic converters can burn through

7. While on the road, check the car's ESP system. Try to find a car park, where you can go for a spin. If the Brake Assist (BAS) light comes on, there is a problem with the ESP. In most cases the ESP sensor of the system just needs a good cleaning. **ETF**

8. Drive the car on an empty road again and brake hard with both hands this time firmly on the steering wheel. If you can hear any knocking sound, the front suspension rubbers need replacement. This is a more common issue with cars over 50,000 mi / 80,000 km. **DTF**

9. Check the tailpipe for soot. If it's oily, it could mean that the rings are worn. **DTF**

10. The SLK can have issues with burned-through catalytic converters and corroded exhaust mufflers. Check also the tailpipe for rust. **DTF**

Roof:

This subject has been covered already in one of the previous chapters, so here are just a few issues to be checked

1. Most importantly, is the vario roof properly functioning? See the chapter vario roof problems. **DTF**

2. If it is, check that the hinges and connections are properly greased or lubricated. **ETF**

3. Hydraulic cylinders are expensive to replace, so check for any oil leaks, if possible also under the headliners (at the front). **DTF**

4. Sometimes the roof is not properly adjusted, which can exhibit itself with paint issues with the rear bumper and the trunk lid – inspect these areas for paint damage. **DTF**

Engine and suspension:

1. Does the exhaust smoke blue, when the engine is running under load (this of course you can only realize, when you have a friend driving behind you). A dealer should check for cylinder leakage or determine, whether valve guides or rings are worn (ask for a compression test). Is there any burning smell under the hood? This could also be caused by some oil runoff, or if the oil pan had been overfilled. Valves and rings are **DTF**

2. Does the exhaust smoke, when you drive the car and then slow down. It could mean that the rings are worn. **DTF**

3. Start the cold engine and have someone close with his hand or a solid object the exhaust tip. Please ensure first that also the exhaust tip is cold, so you do not burn your hand! Have then someone check whether there is any leakage in the engine bay from the exhaust manifold. **DTF**

4. Does the engine run a bit rough? One suspect can be the Mass Air Flow (MAF) sensor. In Kompressor SLKs, the MAF sensor samples incoming air after it has left the charged air cooler on its way to the throttle body. Depending where and how the car has been used, the MAF sensor's probe can become coated in dirt. **ETF**

Check the suspensions for any corrosion. This is mostly on the surface only

5. Any noise from the engine at cold start could come from one of two belt tensioner bearings. **ETF**

6. Check the drive belts for any wear. They should have been replaced on cars with over 60,000 mi / 100,000 km on the clock. **ETF**

7. When was the coolant changed? This should be done at least every three years. If you will do it, buy original coolant from your DB-dealer, it's not expensive. **ETF**

8. Unfasten intake hose to the MAF. If you can see any signs of oil, the oil separator could have a problem. **ETF**

9. Another potential oil leak should be checked at the cam adjuster magnet. It's located under a grey cover in front of the engine. If the leak is bad, have it replaced. Eventually over time it will start to leak again, so as a precautionary method put a blocker in place, as oil from this place can find its way inside the wire and up to the ECU. As many people do not know about this: the blocker is about 6 in long, relatively inexpensive and just plugs into the loom. It's called "Starter Line" in official DB language. The part no. is: 271 150 27 33. **ETF**

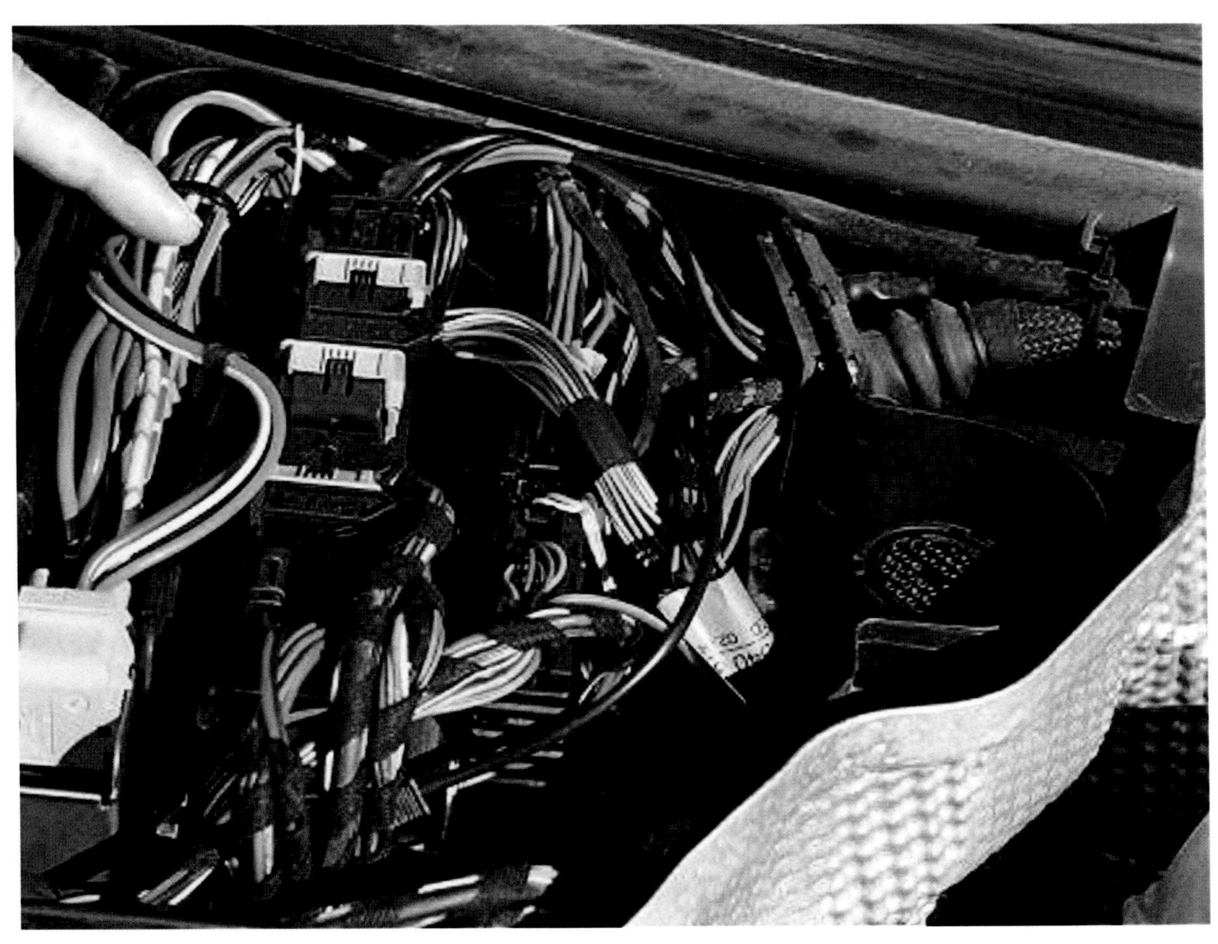

Oil can find its way into the ECU

Check the differential for oil leaks

10. Check for any noises from the supercharger. Any unusual whining could mean you need an expensive replacement. **DTF**

11. Depending on how hard the SLK was driven by its previous owner, at over 50,000 mi / 80,000 km the shock absorbers will be due for a change. So better check them. **ETF**

Transmission:

1. Automatic transmission and rear axle differential should be checked for oil leakage or noise. **DTF**

2. Find out, when transmission fluid had been changed. It should be done every 25,000 mi / 40,000 km, while the engine is warm. **ETF**

3. If the transmission or differential is noisy, this is most often caused by worn or wrongly inflated tires. **ETF**

4. If you want to buy an SLK with manual transmission, this is how to check the clutch: after having started the car, put it in third gear and apply the brakes. Then slowly release the clutch pedal, while still applying the brakes. If the clutch is ok, the car should stall now. If not, the clutch can be worn out and needs replacing. **DTF**

Interior:

1. The biggest issue is usually the center console, where the paint loves to peel off. If you cannot fix this issue yourself, expect the repair to be expensive, as it takes time. If, on the other hand, you trust your DIY capabilities, it is worth going to *YouTube,* where you can find informative videos for this job. **ETF**
2. Drive the car through an automated car wash and check for any leakage from the roof or windows, which could mean you have an issue with the hardtop or the windows do not fit precisely. **DTF**
3. Seats of pre-facelift cars are more prone to wear. Check also leather for wear. Most people will be unable to repair leather properly, so they are better advised to go to a specialist, meaning that issues are **DTF**
4. Do all the gauges function properly. DTF
5. When inside the car, turn all interior lights off. Switch on exterior lights and turn the dimmer switch on the instrument panel to see, whether the instrument lights are working. **ETF**
6. Is the air-con working. **DTF**
7. Check if the air circulation flap works by turning the fan on or off. It is vacuum-assisted and could be perforated. **DTF**

The SLK's VIN explained

The VIN or FIN (as part of the certification tag) is your SLK's unique DNA and can be found on US-bound cars on the builder's plate or verification tag on the driver's door jamb below the lock (see photo below) and on the nearside base of the windscreen in white lettering. On non US-bound cars it is stamped on the top center of the SLK's firewall with the type plate at the passenger's door jamb (see drawing on top of page 132). There you will also find the paint code. On all cars the VIN can also be found in the inner wheel arch on the car's left side, the steering wheel column and of course in your SLK's title, guarantee and maintenance book.

It is always 17 characters long and starts in the case of Daimler-Benz with "WDB". There are differences between the North American VIN's and the one for the rest of the world, sometimes called FIN for "Fahrzeug-Identifikations-Nummer". For simplicity reasons, we will stick here to the name VIN. There is one more way to find out about your specific car's VIN and that is its instrument cluster. Once you have inserted the key, switch it to the ON position. Set the cluster to display km or mph (depending on your location) and press the reset button three times. Go then through the menu until the VIN is being displayed. This code should of course match the other ones.

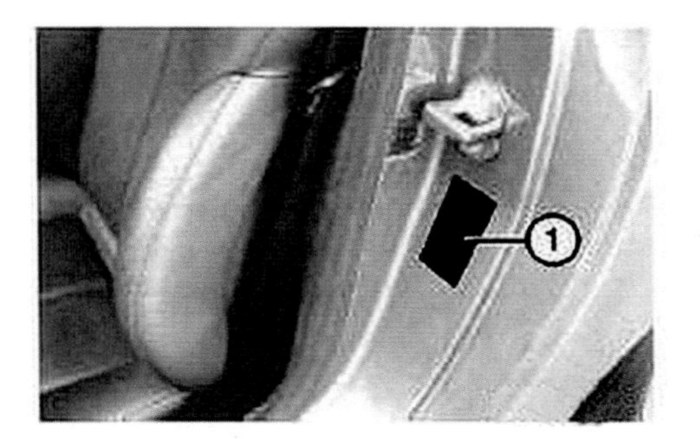

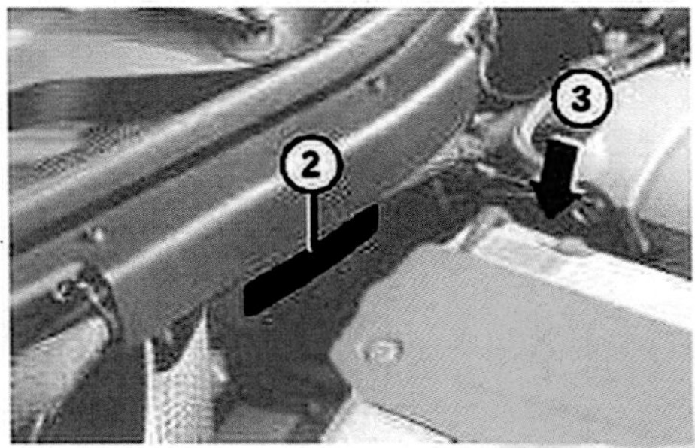

1. Certification label

2. Vehicle Identification Number (VIN)

3. Engine number (engraved on engine)

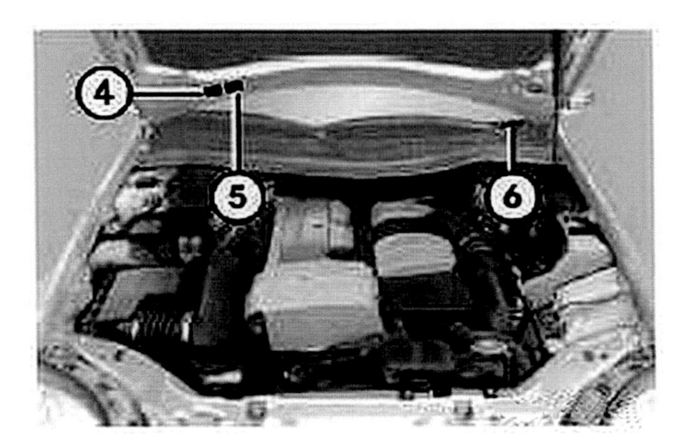

4. Emission Control Label

5. Information label, California version

6. VIN at lower edge of windshield

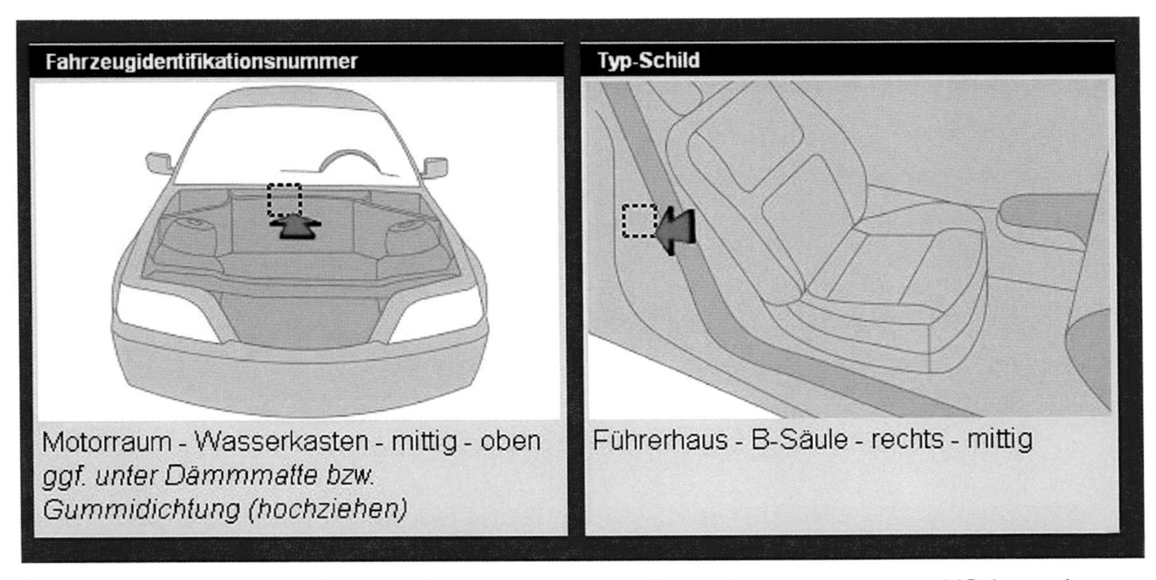

The two drawings show the location of the VIN (left) and body tag on non US-bound cars

This is a certification tag for a US model, a European version will be shown on the next page. All VINs and data card codes are not from actual cars and are for demonstration purpose only

Positions 1-3 identify the manufacturer. In our case it should read WDB, which stands for Daimler-Chrysler. Cars can also show a WDC instead.

Position 4 shows the respective Mercedes model and should read "K" for SLK, the SL R230 reads for example "S".

Position 5 is the respective car's body style. It reads "K" for the SLK as Cabriolet/Roadster or for example "F" in case of a Mercedes sedan.

Positions 6-7 identify the model within the series, in our case it reads 65, so it is a SLK320.

Position 8 is meant for the safety restraint system, which in case of the SLK should read "E" for a car equipped with emergency pre-tensioners and driver/passenger front airbags. In case the car was equipped with additional side airbags, the "E" was replaced with an "F"

Position 9 determines through a somewhat complicated mathematical formula that the previous numbers of the VIN are not fake

Position 10 represents the SLK's model year alpha-numerically. It should not be confused with the year the car was actually delivered or sold. A "W" stands for 1997, while a "X" stands for 1998 and an "Y" for 1999 etc. At the end of the alphabet it all starts with numbers 1-9, so "1" stands for the year 2000 and our "3" shows the production year 2002, which is also shown at the top right side of the plate. After "9" it starts with the alphabet again, so while "9" is used for the year 2008, the "A" stands for 2009 etc.

Position 11 identifies the plant, where the car was manufactured. In our case it should be a letter from "F-H", which indicates for both the SLK and SL the plant in Bremen.

Positions 12-17 indicate the order in which the SLK has left the assembly line. It's also the SLK's chassis number. These last six digits are perhaps the most critical numbers of the VIN. Due to possible mid-year production changes, they are vital in identifying the proper part numbers for ignition, fuel, emission and engine components: Such parts are often listed with the caveat that they fit SLK models up to a particular VIN or before or after a VIN sequence.

The paint number is a three digit code and is for US-bound cars part of the black builder's plate in the door jamb and can be found to the right side of the VIN. In our sample case the color code "960" stands for "Alabaster White Non-Metallic". "040" means "Black", "744" is "Brilliant Silver" for example. Non US-bound cars have the paint code on the body tag

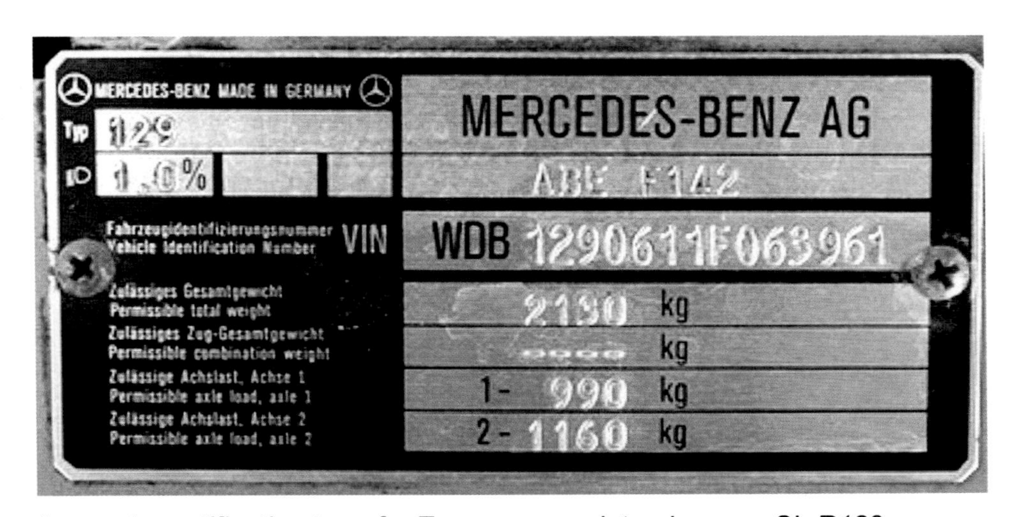

A sample certification tag of a European roadster, here an SL R129

As one can see, VINs for cars outside the US start after the manufacturer code with the type of car. This is repeated on the top left side of the certification tag. The next three digits "061" stand for the model within the car's series, which is in this case the 300SL-24. More explanations on the chassis prefixes one can find on page 135. The next digit is either a "1" as in our case. It stands for a lhd car. A "2" would mean a rhd car. The next following character stipulates in which plant the car was produced. Characters from "A to E" for example would mean Sindelfingen, while "F to H" were used for Bremen. The last six digits indicate again the chassis number and the order in which the car has left the assembly line.

The certification tag does not contain any information regarding the interior or features/extras of the car. There are various sites on the internet, where, after insertion of the VIN, exact data on a particular car's equipment will be given. Information about the paint and a car's specific equipment can usually be found on the data card that came with the car, when it was new. On earlier Mercedes models a plate with respective paint and body information was located prominently on the right side of the radiator cross support.

This chapter is a good place to list the respective numbers of all R170 versions:

1.The SLK200 R170 E20 version, built from April 1996 to Jan. 2000:
Chassis prefix: 170.435, engine M111 E2,0 prefix: 111.946 L4
2.The SLK200K R170 E20 ML version, built from April 1996 to Jan. 2000:
Chassis prefix: 170.444, engine M111 E20 ML, prefix: 111.943 L4
3.The SLK230K R170 E23 ML version, built from April 1996 to Jan. 2000:
Chassis prefix: 170.447, engine M111 E23 ML, prefix: 111.973 L4
4.The SLK200K R170 E20 ML version, built from Jan. 2000 to April 2004:
Chassis prefix: 170.445, engine M111 E20 ML, prefix: 111.985 L4
5.The SLK230K R170 E23 ML version, built from Jan. 2000 to April 2004:
Chassis prefix: 170.449, engine M111 E23 ML, prefix: 111.983 L4
6.The SLK320 R170 E32 version, built from Jan. 2000 to April 2004:
Chassis prefix: 170.465, engine M112 E32, prefix: 112.947 V6
7.The SLK32 AMG R170 E32 ML version, built from Jan. 2000 to April 2004:
Chassis prefix: 170.466, engine M112 E32 ML, prefix: 112.960 V6

The SLK's data card with model code description

The Owner's Manual and Service Booklet should ideally still be with the car, as they contain two Data Cards. One of these cards contains the key codes and should definitely NOT be stored in your car. The second one does not contain this information and should be kept in the car, as it helps the technicians in a service facility to order the correct parts. This Data Card has codes for the original equipment and additional extras that came with the car. Everything printed on it is in German, so it offers some translations and space for the owner to write down his name etc. If the car`s Data Card is lost, one of the Daimler-Benz or previously mentioned R170-enthusiast websites could be of assistance. Search those sites for keywords such as "Factory Option Codes" or "Data Card". That will lead you to fellow enthusiasts, who might be able to help with retrieving the Data Codes from the VIN of your car. Another option to retrieve those data can be a drive to your DB-dealer or Mercedes specialist shop.

Knowing with what options your car had left the assembly line might be helpful, when ordering parts for it. Sometimes you will find that the optional extras, your SLK should have come with, are no longer installed. One example is the CD changer. Even when there is none available, a quick look behind the car's right trunk paneling might reveal its harnesses, so a replacement could be fairly simple.

2 WARTUNGSHEFT

1	Mercedes-Benz	11 Reifen vorn 1	PIRELLI	21 Achse vorn 1		31 Lack/L.-Zus.1	040
2 Fg.-Nr.	Fahrzeugdaten	12 Reifen vorn 2		22 Achse vorn 2		32 Lack/L.-Zus.2	
WDB	170444 1F 147065 4	13 Reifen hint. 1		23 Achse hint. 1		33 Lack/L.-Zus.3	
3 Motor-Nr.	111958 12 004322	14 Reifen hint. 2		24 Achse hint. 2		34 Lack/L.-Zus.4	
4 Typ	SLK 200 KOMPRESSOR	15 Heizung		25 Aufbau/Fahrerhaus		35 Lack/L.-Zus.5	
5 Auftrags-Nr.	0 9 221 23442	16 Felgen		26 Pritsche		36 Türschloß	
6 Produkt.-Nr.	2886102 3	17 Leuchten	BOSCH	27 VIN		37 Lenkschloß	
7 Getriebe	722616 0 2120270	18 Scheibenwisch.		28 Anh.-Kuppl.		38 Getriebeschloß	
8 Vert. Getriebe		19 Seilwinde		29 Lenkung		39 Tankschloß	
9 Nebenantrieb		20 Wegdrehz.-A.		30 Ausstattung	211	40 Retarder	

309 330 423 580 648 726 756 801 810 873 926 988 N80 N96

The upper part of the data card carries 40 number spaces and as one can see, very few of them are filled out. Daimler-Benz data cards changed their appearance over the past decades frequently, for example, a card from a 1971 R107 SL looks vastly different from the one of a 1987 R107 SL.

As the codes in this data card might be a bit difficult to read, we will look at it box by box. We start with the upper part, left side:

WDB	170444 1F 147065
3 Motor-Nr.	111958 12 004322
4 Typ	SLK 200 KOMPRESSOR
5 Auftrags-Nr.	0 9 221 23442
6 Produkt.-Nr.	2886102 3
7 Getriebe	722616 0 2120270
8 Vert. Getriebe	
9 Nebenantrieb	

The VIN has already been dealt with in the previous chapter and does not need to be explained here one more time.

Box 3 covers the "Motor-Nr." or engine number, which follows more or less the same logic as the chassis number/VIN. "111" was used for the type of engine and "958" for the version of that particular power plant. Our sample M111 power plant was used in various configurations for some ten different Mercedes cars from the W202 C-class to the W901 Sprinter Van. It even made it into a Volkswagen Van, called the "LT". So, in case your SLK had an engine change, it does not hurt to have a careful check, what type of M111 (or any other engine you have) has been planted into its engine bay.

The seventh digit identifies lhd cars with a "1" and rhd cars with a "2", while the eighth digit shows a "0" for manual or "2" for automatic transmission. The last six digits show that in our case the engine was the 4,322th one produced. They are sequential by transmission type, so are counted separately for manual and automatic versions.

Box 5 deals with the "Auftrags-Nr" or order no. It is one of the most interesting codes of the data card and consists of ten digits. The first digit shows the month, the second one the last digit of the year the car was ordered.

For some reason the first digit is rarely used. The second digit "9" means that our sample SLK200 was ordered in 1999.

The next three digits show, which dealer/country has placed the order for our car. If the code starts with a "2" or "3", it shows that the car was ordered by a Mercedes subsidiary (or its affiliate) in Germany. Then the following two digits determine together with the "2" the region and dealer. In our case the SLK was ordered in Cologne (Köln). In case of places outside Germany, a "5" as first digit means countries in other parts of Europe. A "537" means the UK, "531" France, "577" Spain or "543" Italy for example.

Countries in the Americas start with a "7". If followed by "03" to "07" they were destined for the US (for a short time, codes 708 to 718 were also used for the US). An interesting number is "707" as it means that this particular car was bought through the European Delivery Program. In the 1960s over one third of all Mercedes sold in the US were bought through this program, where the future owner picked up his car in Stuttgart-Sindelfingen. He/she then usually drove it through parts of Europe, before the new car was shipped to its final destination in the US. Nowadays this rarely (if at all) happens. Cars built for use in Canada used code "701" or, if such a car was for European Delivery, you'd see code "702". The Oceania region starts with a "9" (901 for Australia, 919 for NZ), while markets in Asia have an "8" as first of these three digits (Japan: 839, Hong Kong: 823).

The remaining four digits are sequential for that particular region/dealer and that year. In case of our R170 it means that it was in 1999 the 23,442nd car ordered (again, this number is fictitious and should just demonstrate its purpose).

Box 6 indicates the "Prod.-Nr." or "Produktions-Nummer", which is the car's production number

Box 7 shows the transmission number, which is also stamped inside the bell-housing

The remaining boxes are of minor interest for the SLK, but just to make this description complete, they have the following meaning:

Box 8: Verteilergetriebe: Transfer transmission

Box 9: Nebenantrieb: auxiliary or second drive (used for example with 4-matic)

Box 11 to 14: Reifen vorn/hint.: tires front and rear

Box 15: Heizung: heating system

Box 16: Felgen: rims

Box 17: Leuchten: headlamps (usually Bosch and Hella)

Box 18: Scheibenwischer: windshield-wipers (usually Bosch)

Box 19: Seilwinde: cable winch

Box 20: Wegdrehz-A or "Wegdrehzahl-Anzeige" (in English it means "speedometer"). This particular word was used in the German language in the 1950s, where no car except the 300SL/190SL had anything as fancy as a speedo. For the last couple of decades it is called "Drehzahlmesser"

21 Achse vorn 1		31 Lack/L-Zus.1	040
22 Achse vorn 2		32 Lack/L-Zus.2	
23 Achse hint. 1		33 Lack/L-Zus.3	
24 Achse hint. 2		34 Lack/L-Zus.4	
25 Aufbau/ Fahrerhaus		35 Lack/L-Zus.5	
26 Pritsche		36 Türschloß	
27 VIN		37 Lenkschloß	
28 Anh.-Kuppl.		38 Getriebeschloß	
29 Lenkung		39 Tankschloß	
30 Ausstattung	211	40 Retarder	

Box 21 to 24: Achse vorn/hint. Axle front and rear

Box 25: Aufbau/Fahrerhaus. This and the next box show that Daimler AG is also the manufacturer of trucks, as this refers to the cabin of a van/truck and stands for: body/cabin

Box 26: Pritsche: berth or platform of a van/truck

Box 27: VIN

Box 28: Anh.-Kuppl. or "Anhänger-Kupplung": tow bar

Box 29: Lenkung: steering

Box 30: Austattung: interior trim code. In our sample case "211" stands for black (sometimes anthracite) leather interior

Box 31 to 35: Lack-Zus1 or "Lack-Zusammensetzung 1": paint-composition 1. The reason for giving the paint so much room in five boxes is its more diverse presentation on modern cars. Our sample car has color code "040" black

Box 36 to 39 offer the key codes for doors, steering, transmission and fuel cap

Box 40: Retarder: this function is most probably used on large trucks, as it replaces/eases certain functions of the primary friction-based breaking system

8 Vert. Getriebe | 19 Seilwinde | 29 Lenkung
9 Nebenantrieb | 20 Wegdrehz.-A. | 30 Ausstattung 211

309 330 423 580 648 726 756 801 810 873 926 988 N80 N96

The three digit codes that can be found below those are of equal importance as they define the options that came with your specific SLK (and any other Mercedes as a matter of fact), when it left the assembly line. It was easy for North America, Australia and Japan and a few other markets, where the SLK came almost fully equipped with just five options to choose from. But the situation was very much different for Europe for example, where the car came standard with fabric seats, no air-con or adjustable steering column to name just three. Without going too much into the details (the following list can do this better for any specific car), there are a few options that need to be explained, as they do not relate entirely to the car, but also the country it was shipped to.

One such option is code “461”, which means that the car came equipped for markets such as the US and UK with instruments with English lettering and mileage reading. In case of the US, this would be followed by “494”, a code used for the US and Canada (Canada of course did not have code “461”). The country code in this options list is different from the one used in the order number in the card’s upper portion, where the US has country codes from 701 to 708! The option code for the UK is “622” and for Australia “625”.

Model code description

The following list might be a bit long, but it covers all options that were available for the R170. With regards to country codes, the author has only listed the codes for the major countries, in order not to make this list too exhaustive. It is interesting that some of the countries are hidden between car specific options. 675L covers for example South Africa, while the next following code 685U covers the color option Yellowstone. Or 816U is the code for Andradite Green Metallic, while the next following code 823L is meant for Hong Kong.

The code system comes in three parts. The first one has only numbers and deals in general mostly with technical equipment, the second part has numbers, followed by a letter and covers most of the paints. The third part starts with a letter, followed by numbers, it covers equipment parts such as Designo, special wheels etc. But don't be surprised to find also technical extras under the last part or Designo extras in the first part. The three parts are separated by R170 photos.

003 CONSTRUCTION SEQUENCE
004 AV VEHICLE
005 TEST DEPT. UNTERTUERKHEIM, TRIAL
006 EXPERIMENTAL, PRESS / TEST
007 TEST DEPT. SINDELFINGEN, BODYWORK DEVELOPMENT
008 NEAR-LAUNCH ROAD TRIALS, FLEET UNTERTUERKHEIM /TRI
009 PHOTO
010 ROAD TEST W50
011 ROAD TEST W67
012 TRAINING / DIAGNOSIS VP/S
013 EXHIBITION (IF NOT CODE 997)
014 NEAR-LAUNCH ROAD TRIALS, FLEET SINDELFINGEN/W54 RA
015 KD – EQUIPMENT
016 FIELD TEST INLAND/EXPORT
017 NON CUSTOMER READY VEHICLE
018 CUSTOMER READY VEHICLES WHICH SHOULD BE MODIFIED
019 FIELD TEST VEHICLES, DEMONSTRATION VEHICLES (CUSTO

020 DEMONSTRATION VEHICLE, SALES
021 DESIGNO - LEATHER
022 DESIGNO - DECORATIVE TRIM
024 QM RELEASE VEHICLES
026 DISCONTINUATION OF SPARE KEY
029 PRICE CONTROL AUTOMATIC TRANSMISION (210 E28/E32)
030 AMG - MAJOR ASSEMBLY V8-M55/V12-M60
031 CONVERSION OF CNS TO ICS (MODEL SERIES 140, JAPAN)
032 TAIWAN - GERAEUSCHTEST GETRIEBE
034 PRICE CONTROL CHANGE RADIO CLASSIC -> SPECIAL
038 ESSAI EN SERIE DE32LA
039 PRODUCTION TEST M111 EVO/BITURBO M275/OM613 MOD.
044 REGULATION WASHER SYSTEM
045 STEUERCODE BIGGER BATTERY BR 209
047 CONTROL-CODE USA
049 MSM2 ENGINE CONTROL
050 YEAR OF MODIFICATION 99/2
058 YEAR OF MODIFICATION 97/2
059 AEJ.98/2
110 FUEL AMOUNT FOR COLLECTION BY CUSTOMER
170 ENGINE OUTPUT, FRONT
185 PARTS NOT ON ORIGINAL PARTS LIST FOR 4MATIC M112
197 REPOSITION EMO
202 OWNERS MANUAL AND SERVICE RECORD - GERMAN
205 OWNERS MANUAL AND SERVICE RECORD - ENGLISH
206 OWNERS MANUAL AND SERVICE RECORD - ITALIAN
207 OWNERS MANUAL AND SERVICE RECORD - FRENCH
208 OWNER'S MANUAL AND SERVICE BOOKLET - SPANISH
209 OWNER'S MANUAL AND SERVICE BOOKLET - PORTUGUESE
212 ELECTRONIC TRACTION SYSTEM (ETS)
221 LEFT FRONT SEAT, ELECTRICALLY ADJUSTABLE
222 RIGHT FRONT SEAT, ELECTRICALLY ADJUSTABLE
231 GARAGE DOOR OPENER
232 GARAGE DOOR OPENER WITH 284 - 390 MHZ FREQUENCY
236 SPECIAL LAMP SWITCHING - DAYTIME RUNNING LAMPS
244 SPORTS SEATS
249 INSIDE AND OUTSIDE MIRROR AUTOMATIC DIMMING
251 RADIO MB - EXQUISIT - USA
253 RADIO MB - EXQUISIT - JAPAN
254 RADIO MB AUDIO 30 - USA
255 RADIO MB AUDIO 30 - JAPAN
260 TYPE DESIGNATION ON TRUNK LID - DELITION
261 TYPE DESIGNATION ON FENDER / SIDEWARD DELETION
263 LICENSE PLATE ATTACHMENT ASIA / MEXICO
264 LICENSE PLATE ATTACHMENT AMERICA
270 INVALID/ANTENNA F.D-NET TELEPHONE ON FENDER REAR.L

271 T.PHONE PRE-INSTALLN.COMPL.D-NET MOBILE ON TOWER
272 PHONE PREINST. NON-NETWORKED INCL. PHONE ANTENNA
273 TELEPHONE PRE-INSTALLATION D-NET MOBILE
278 TELEPHONE PRE-INSTALLATION COMPL. D-NET
292 SIDEBAG
309 CUP HOLDER
312 TELEPHONE D-NET "MOBILE" AT TOWER (NOKIA 3110)
313 CHARGING STATION FOR CELL PHONE
314 TELEPHONE D-NET STANDARD
315 PHONECARD D1 DEBITEL (PRICE REDUCTION)
316 INVALID/ TELEPHONE (D2B) CENTER CONSOLE (MOTOROLA)
317 TELEPHONE (D2B) HANDY IN CENTRAL CONSOLE
328 PHONECARD D2 DEBITEL (PRICE REDUCTION)
329 TELEPHONE PRE-INSTALLATION AMPS
330 CD COMPARTMENT
331 CASSETTE COMPARTMENT
343 AIR FILTER
349 PREP. FOR EMERGENCY CALL SYSTEM
351 AUTOMOTIVE PILOT-SYSTEM (APS)
353 AUDIO 30 APS
361 LOADING COSTS (MACHINE FORMATION ON FA 2)
363 INCOMPLETE DELIVERY SLIP (FOR SAS AND KWS)
364 RETRO TIRE CHANGE
365 REMOVAL COSTS FOR CODE 668
367 REMOVAL COSTS FOR CODE 524 AND 668
368 INSTALLATION COSTS FOR CODE 524
369 INSTALLATION COSTS FOR CODE 524 AND 668
370 INSTALLATION COSTS FOR CODE 668
423 5-SPEED AUTOMATIC TRANSMISSION
441 STEERING COLUMN, ADJUSTABLE
460 VEHICLES FOR CANADA, ADDITIONAL PARTS
461 INSTRUMENT WITH MILES IND. AND ENGLISH LEGEND
471 ACCELERATION SKID CONTROL (ASR)
472 ELECTRONIC STABILITY PROGRAM (ESP)
481 UNDERSHIELDS
494 U.S. VERSION
498 JAPAN VERSION
500 OUTSIDE REAR VIEW MIRROR LH AND RH FOLDING
510 MB RADIO EXQUISIT WITH VK, RDS (BECKER)
511 RADIO MB EXQUISIT WITH VK, RDS (PANASONIC)
512 MB RADIO SPECIAL WITH TRAFF. MESS. RDS
515 MB RADIO CLASSIC WITH TRAFF. MESS, RDS
516 RADIO MB CLASSIC WITHOUT TRAFFIC NEWS DECODER (VK)
518 RADIO MB EXQUISIT WITHOUT TRAFFIC NEWS DECODER, WI
524 PAINTWORK - PRESERVATION
533 SPEAKERS FRONT AND REAR - WITHOUT RADIO

551 ANTI-THEFT/ANTI-BREAK-IN WARNING SYSTEM
552 THEFT WARNING SYSTEM FOR SWITZERLAND
560 ELECTRIC. ADJUSTABLE DRIVER SEAT L. AND R.
580 AIRCONDITIONER
600 HEADLAMPS - CLEANING EQUIPMENT
602 CUSTOMS LICENSE PLATE FIXTURE
612 HEADLAMP-XENON R.H.TRAFFIC
613 HEADLAMP LEFT-HAND TRAFFIC
617 XENON HEADLAMPS, LEFT-HAND TRAFFIC
623 VERSION FOR THE GULF STATES
625 VERSION FOR AUSTRALIA
630 ECE - WARNING TRIANGLE
634 DELETION - FIRST AID KIT
636 DELETION - WARNING TRIANGLE
642 INVALID/L.A.WHEELS, 7-HOLE: FR. 7X16 / REAR 8X16
645 WINTER TIRES M + S
648 INVALID/L.A.WHEELS 6-HOLE: FR. 7X16 / REAR 8X16
658 LIGHT ALLOY WHEELS EVO-DESIGN
668 PACKAGING FOR SHIPPING VEHICLES WITH TIE-DOWN HOOK
669 SPARE WHEEL / FOLDING WHEEL
673 HIGH-CAPACITY BATTERY
682 FIREEXTINGUISHER
687 MODEL YEAR ON TYPE LABEL
688 INVALID/L.A.5-SPOKE DESIGN, 16" WITH MIXED TIRES
689 L.A. 7-SPOKE DESIGN, 17 INCH WITH MIXED TIRES
726 PRE-EQUIPMENT FOR ROOF SUPPORT SYSTEM
732 WOOD VERSION, BIRD'S EYE MAPLE BLACK/ANTHRACITE
734 WOOD DESIGN EUCALYPTUS-RIEGEL INCL. STG.WHL
750 MB AUDIO 30 RADIO WITH VK/RDS
752 RADIO MB AUDIO 30 WITHOUT VK/RDS
753 RADIO MB AUDIO 10 CC WITH VK/RDS
754 RADIO MB AUDIO 10 CC WITHOUT VK/RDS
755 RADIO MB SPECIAL SINGLE CD
756 RADIO MB AUDIO 10 CD WITH VK/RDS
761 RADIO RC W. REDUCED RANGE W/O PANIC (315 MHZ)
762 RADIO REMOTE CONTROL W/O PANIC SWITCH (315 MHZ)
763 RADIO REMOTE CONTROL W/ PANIC SWITCH (315 MHZ)
767 AMG DISK WHEEL 17 INCH WITH MIXED TIRES
772 AMG STYLING PACKAGE-FRONT SPOILER, SIDE SKIRT
794 AMG-WHEELS 7,5 X 17 SQUEEZE-IN DEPTH 37 VA 225/45
800 YEAR OF MODIFICATION 99/1
801 AEJ 00/1 R 170 AEJ 99/2
802 AEJ 01/1/X
803 AEJ 02/1/2/X
804 AEJ 03/1; 03/X
807 AEJ 06/1/M/X

808 AEJ 07/1
809 AEJ 08/1
810 SOUND SYSTEM
817 ALARM SIREN FOR THEFT WARNING SYSTEM
819 CD CHANGER
820 VEHICLES FOR TOURIST
822 VEHICLES FOR SOUTH-AFRIKA, ADDITIONAL PARTS
823 VEHICLES FOR SWITZERLAND, ADDITIONAL PARTS
825 VEHICLES FOR SWEDEN, ADDITIONAL PARTS
826 VEHICLES FOR FRANCE, ADDITIONAL PARTS
828 CATALYST COATING - DELETION
829 VEHICLES FOR NORWAY, ADDITIONAL PARTS
830 CHINA-VEHICLES-ADDITIONAL PARTS
831 VERSION FOR ITALY SUPPLEMENTARY PARTS
832 VEHICLES FOR DENMARK, ADDITIONAL PARTS
833 INVALID/GREATBRITAIN, ADDITIONAL PARTS
835 SOUTHERN KOREA-SUPPLEMENTARY PARTS
850 TRIAL UT, TYPE TEST/CERTIFICATION
852 MOBILE.PRE-INSTALL.COMPL.ON TOWER NOKIA SERIES 5/6
853 TELEPHONE FITTED ON "TOWER"; NOKIA, D-NET
854 TELEPHONE "CELL PHONE", NOKIA 6210/6310I
859 CTEL CARD E-NETWORK DEBITEL (PRICE REDUCTION)
860 TV-TUNER ANALOG
873 SEAT HEATER FOR LEFT AND RIGHT FRONT SEATS
875 HEATED SCREEN WASH SYSTEM
882 INTERIOR SAFEGUARD
911 NOTE FOR SPECIAL EQUIPMENT (PRESS VEHICLES)
913 AIR-CONDITIONING SYSTEM FOR HOT COUNTRIES
914 BRAKE ASSIST (BAS)
916 VEHICLES FOR HOT COUNTRIES - ADDITIONAL PARTS
918 EMISSION CONTROL SYSTEM UNREGULATED
923 EMISSION CONTROL D3-MEASURES
926 EXHAUST GAS CLEANING WITH EU4 TECHNOLOGY (EURO 4)
980 REG. DOC. AND ABE NO. ON TYPE LABEL FOR EXPORT
981 REG. DOC. OMISSION AND NO ABE NO. ON TYPE LABEL
982 VEHICLES FOR FINLAND, ADDITIONAL PARTS
983 COC PAPER EU4 TECHN. + NO VEH. TITLE OF OWNERSHIP
984 COC DOC., DELETION OF VEHICLE REGISTRATION DOC.
985 REG.DOC. AND COC DOC. EU4 TECHNOLOGY
986 IDENTIFICATIONNUMBER (VIN-NO.)
987 BATTERY ISOLATION SWITCH FOR SHIPMENT VEHICLES
988 VEH. TIT. OF OWN. & COC DOC. + MODEL PLATE (MACH.)
989 IDENTIFICATIONLABELUNDERWINDSHIELD
994 STATIONARY CAR FOR USE ON EXHIBITION
997 STATIONARY CAR FOR USE ON EXHIBITION

000A UPHOLSTERY FABRIC
008U DESIGNOALLANITEGREEN
010A FABRIC DUNE
011A FABRIC MESCALERO /DUNE ANTHRACITE
012A FABRIC, DUNE, MERLIN BLUE
015U DESIGNO-PURPLE PAINT
017A FABRIC DUNE MAGMA RED
017U DESIGNO-VARIOCOLOR-PAINTING
01Q LARGE TRIAL FUELPUMP
020U DESIGNO-ORANGE PAINT
021A CLOTH BLACK
021U DESIGNO-LCP PAINTWORK
022A CLOTH BLUE MONDRIAN
022U DESIGNO-BROWN BLACK PAINT
023U DESIGNO - VARICOLOR 2 PAINTWORK
024U DESIGNO-LIGHT GREEN PAINT
025U DESIGNO-BRILLIANT BLACK PAINT
026A CLOTH MINT
026U DESIGNO - SEA BLUE PAINTWORK
027A CLOTH SCARLAT
027U DESIGNO-LCP PAINTWORK
029U DESIGNO-SILVER PAINTWORK

030U DESIGNO-YELLOW GOLD PAINTWORK
031U DESIGNO-CHROMAFLAIR 1 PAINTWORK
032U DESIGNO-MYSTIC CLUE PAINTWORK
033U DESIGNO-MOCCA BLACK PAINTWORK
034U DESIGNO VARICOLOR 3 PAINT COATS
036U DESIGNO VARICOLOR 4 PAINT COATS
037U DESIGNO MYSTIC RED PAINT
040U BLACK
041U DESIGNO GRAPHITE GREEN PAINT
143U NEVE WHITE
149U POLAR WHITE
170D SPRINGS IN ACCORDANCE WITH EDP - PROGRAM
170E ERPROBUNGSFAHRZEUG 170 - TA8376
170G LARGE SCALE PRODUCTION TEST
170K CUSTOMER REQUEST
170P SELECTION PACKAGE
170S UNCODED SPECIAL VERSIONS
170V TEST PARTS LIST
170Z INTERMEDIATE VERSION
189U GREEN BLACK METALLIC
197U OBSIDIAN BLACK
200A LEATHER
200B OWNERS MANUAL AND SERVICE RECORD - DANISH
201B OWNERS MANUAL AND SERVICE RECORD - DUTCH
202B OWNERS MANUAL AND SERVICE RECORD - GERMAN
203B OWNERS MANUAL AND SERVICE RECORD - RUSSIAN
204B OWNERS MANUAL AND SERVICE RECORD - FINNISH
205B OWNERS MANUAL AND SERVICE RECORD - ENGLISH
206B OWNERS MANUAL AND SERVICE RECORD - ITALIAN
207B OWNERS MANUAL AND SERVICE RECORD - FRENCH
208B OWNERS MANUAL AND SERVICE RECORD - SPANISH
209B OWNERS MANUAL AND SERVICE RECORD - PORTUGESE
210A LEATHER
210B OWNERS MANUAL AND SERVICE RECORD - SWEDISH
211A LEATHER ANTHRACITE
211B OWNERS MANUAL AND SERVICE RECORD - ARABIC
212A LEATHER GALAXY BLUE/MERLIN BLUE
212B OWNERS MANUAL AND SERVICE RECORD - AMERICAN
215A LEATHER QUARTZ/SIAM BEIGE
217A LEATHER MAGMA RED
218A LEATHER GREY
219A LEATHER LOTUS YELLOW
220B INFO PLATE, COOLANT - GERMAN
221A LEATHER BLACK
221B SIGN COOLANT/REFUELING - ENGLISH
222A LEATHER TWO-COLOR (BLUE)

222B INFO PLATE COOLANT/REFUELING - FRENCH
223B INFO PLATE FOR COOLANT - SPANISH
225A LEATHER QUARTZ
227A LEATHER TWO-COLOR (RED)
230B CUSTOMER SERVICE - STATION EUROPE
231B CUSTOMER SERVICE - STATION LATIN AMERICA
232B CUSTOMER SERVICE - STATION ASIA WITH ISRAEL
233B CUSTOMER SERVICE - STATION ASIA WITHOUT ISRAEL
234B CUSTOMER SERVICE - STATION AFRICA
235B CUSTOMER SERVICE - STATION AUSTRALIA
236B WITHOUT CUSTOMER SERVICE - STATION INDEX
250B MOBILO LIFE/EUROPE SERVICE PACKAGE
252U DESIGNO-GREEN PAINT
279U VIVIANITE GREEN MET.
2XXL FEDERAL REPUBLIC OF GERMANY
352U LINARITE BLUE - METALLIC PAINT
372U LAZULITHE BLUE - METALLIC PAINT
401L NATO SALES
478U DESIGNO-BROWN PAINT
513L BELGIUM
531L FRANCE
532L FRANCE
535L GREECE
536L GREAT BRITAIN
537L GREAT BRITAIN
536L GREAT BRITAIN
537L GREAT BRITAIN
548U AMBER RED METALLIC
584U PYROPE RED METALLIC FINISH
586U MAGMA-RED - NON-METALLIC PAINTURE
590U FIRE OPAL RED - UNILAC
672L SOUTH AFRICAN REPUBLIC/VEHICLES
674L REPUBLIC OF SOUTH AFRICA
675L REPUBLIC OF SOUTH AFRICA
685U YELLOWSTONE
744U BRILLIANT SILVER METALLIC
7XXL NORTH AND SOUTH AMERICA
810U PRISMA GREEN METALLIC
816U ANDRADITE GREEN METALLIC
823L HONGKONG
825L INDIA
837L ISRAEL
860A LEATHER, NAPPA
861A LEATHER NAPPA BLACK
867A LEATHER NAPPA RED
873L SAUDI ARABIA

875L SINGAPORE
880A LEATHER AMG
881A LEATHER AMG ANTHRACITE/ANTHRACITE
887A LEATHER AMG ANTHRACITE/MAGMA RED
888A LEATHER AMG ANTHRACITE/ALPACA GRAY
8XXL ASIA
960U ALABASTER WHITE - NON METALLIC
9XXL AUSTRALIA / PACIFIC

E003 ADDITIONAL MIRROR OUTSIDE LEFT
E004 ADDITIONAL MIRROR OUTSIDE RIGHT
E012 BICYCLECARRIERLEANLINE
E031 LUGGAGE BOX
E052 SKI CARRIER SWIVEL-MOUNTED
E071 BASIC CARRIER ALUSTYLE
F170 SERIES PRODUCTION 170
FR ROADSTER
GA AUTOMATIC TRANSMISSION
GM MANUAL TRANSMISSION
HA REAR AXLE
J48 CONTROL CODE RASTATT/MERCOSUL PLANT
K01 CONTROL CODE FOR ALARM SIREN (FREQUENCY)
K02 CONTROL CODE FOR ALARM SIREN (FREQUENCY)
K06 EXHAUST CONTROL CODE FOR FTP75
K08 RADIO FREQUENCIES FOR SOUTH AMERICA
170 L LEFT-HAND STEERING
M001 ENGINES WITH SUPERCHARGER

M010 EVO/VEHICLEUPGRADEENGINES
M111 R4-GASOLINE ENGINE M111
M112 V6-GASOLINE ENGINE M112
M20 DISPLACEMENT 2.0 LITER
M23 CAPACITY 2.3 LITRE
M32 CAPACITY 3.2 LITER
P26 SPECIAL MODEL R 170 USA
P29 SPECIAL MODEL - "FINAL EDITION"
P43 SPECIAL EDITION SPECIAL MODEL
Q47 GV - VERKLEIDUNG MOTORRAUM
Q77 OP. TEST, CLUTCH ASSY VST A 017 250 30 01
R RIGHT-HAND STEERING
R01 SUMMER TYRES
R02 INVALID/LIGHT ALLOY RIM
R05 UNG/LM-ALU-RAD 17" CELAENO
U06 EXTERNAL MIRROR FOR INDIA
U12 FLOOR MATS, VELOURS
VL FRONT AXLE HALF, LEFT
VR FRONT AXLE HALF, RIGHT
W50 TRIM PARTS CINNAMORRA DESIGNO
W51 TRIM PARTS CINNAMORRA DESIGNO NATURAL
W52 TRIM PARTS CINNAMORRA DESIGNO ANTHRACITE
X00 LEATHER, DESIGNO, UNI-COLOR
X02 LEATHER, DESIGNO-ULTRA MARINE, UNI-COLOR
X03 LEATHER, DESIGNO-BLUE,UNI-COLOR
X04 LEATHER, DESIGNO-RED, UNI-COLOR
X05 LEATHER, DESIGNO-ORANGE, UNI-COLOR
X07 LEATHER, DESIGNO-PURPLE, UNI-COLOR
X08 LEATHER, DESIGNO-GREEN, UNI-COLOR
X09 LEATHER, DESIGNO-DARK BLUE, UNI-COLOR
X10 DESIGNO SAND SINGLE-COLOR LEATHER
X11 LEATHER, DESIGNO-BLACK,UNI-COLOR
X12 DESIGNO PASTEL YELLOW SINGLE-COLOR LEATHER
X13 DESIGNO MYSTIC RED SINGLE-COLOR LEATHER
X14 DESIGNO GRAPHITE GREEN SINGLE-COLOR LEATHER
X22 LEATHER, DESIGNO-ANTHRACITE, UNI-COLOR
X23 LEATHER, DESIGNO-YELLOWSTONE, UNI-COLOR
X24 LEATHER, DESIGNO-IMPERIAL RED, UNI-COLOR
X25 LEATHER, DESIGNO-VIVIANITEGREEN, UNI-COLOR
X26 LEATHER, DESIGNO-LINARITEBLUE, UNI-COLOR
X31 LEATHER, DESIGNO-DARK GREEN, UNI-COLOR
X33 LEATHER, DESIGNO-MINERALGREEN, UNI-COLOR
X34 LEATHER, DESIGNO-DARK BROWN, UNI-COLOR
X35 LEATHER, DESIGNO-LIGHT BROWN, UNI-COLOR
X38 LEATHER, DESIGNO-SILVER ONE COLOR
X39 LEATHER, DESIGNO-YELLOW GOLD 1 COLOR

X40 LEATHER, DESIGNO-MYSTIC BLUE 1 COLOR
X41 LEATHER, DESIGNO-BORDEAUX RED 1 COLOR
X43 ONE-COLORED DESIGNO LEATHER, LAVA RED
X430 REAR BUMPER ANTEENA F.CARPHONE D-NET
X44 MEDIUM GRAY UNICOLORED DESIGNO LEATHER
X45 DESIGNO COPPER/DARK BROWN SINGLE-COLOR LEATHER
X46 MARINE BLUE UNICOLORED DESIGNO LEATHER
X50 LEATHER, DESIGNO, TWO-COLOR
X51 LEATHER, DESIGNO-GREEN, TWO-COLOR
X52 LEATHER, DESIGNO-BLUE, TWO-COLOR
X53 LEATHER, DESIGNO-ORANGE, TWO-COLOR
X54 LEATHER, DESIGNO-PURPLE, TWO-COLOR
X55 LEATHER, DESIGNO-ULTRA MARINE, TWO-COLOR
X56 LEATHER, DESIGNO-DARK BLUE, TWO-COLOR
X57 LEATHER, DESIGNO-LINARITE BLUE, TWO-COLOR
X58 LEATHER, DESIGNO-YELLOWSTONE, TWO-COLOR
X59 LEATHER, DESIGNO-DARK GREEN, TWO-COLOR
X60 LEATHER, DESIGNO-VIVIANITE GREEN, TWO-COLOR
X61 LEATHER, DESIGNO-MINERAL GREEN, TWO-COLOR
X62 LEATHER, DESIGNO-RED, TWO-COLOR
X63 LEATHER DESIGNO-LIGHT BROWN TWO-COLOR
X64 LEATHER DESIGNO-DARK BROWN TWO-COLOR
X65 LEATHER DESIGNO-ANTHRAZITE TWO-COLOR
X68 LEATHER DESIGNO-SILVER TWO COLOR
X69 LEATHER DESIGNO-YELLOW GOLD 2 COLOR
X70 LEATHER DESIGNO-MYSTIC BLUE TWO COLOR
X71 LEATHER DESIGNO-BORDEAX RED TWO COLOR
X73 DOUBLE-COLORED DESIGNO LEATHER, LAVA RED
X74 MEDIUM GRAY TWO SHADE DESIGNO LEATHER
X75 COPPER TWO SHADE DESIGNO LEATHER
X76 MARINE BLUE TWO SHADE DESIGNO LEATHER
X77 DESIGNO SAND TWO-TONE LEATHER
X78 DESIGNO PASTEL YELLOW TWO-TONE LEATHER
X79 DESIGNO MYSTIC RED TWO-TONE LEATHER
X80 DESIGNO GRAPHITE GREEN TWO-COLOR LEATHER
Y92 TRIM SELECT/SHIFTLEVER, STG.WHL. CINNAMORRA DESIGNO
Y94 SELECTOR LEVER IN LEATHER-/DESIGNO-WOOD VERSION
Y95 STEERING WHEEL IN LEATHER-/DESIGNO-WOOD DESIGN
Y96 2-TONE DES. LEATHER ST. WH.+ DES. LEATHER SEL. LEV.
Y97 TRIM PARTS, IN DESIGNO-COLOR, LEATHER-COVERED
Y98 ROLL-OVER BAR, IN DESIGNO-COLOR, LEATHER-COVERED
Y981 CLEAR WINDSHIELD ASSEMBLY WITH RAIN SENSOR
Y99 SPORTS SEAT INCL.LEATHER DESIGNO TWO-COLORED
Z97 PAINTWORK DESIGNO
Z98 PAINTWORK OUTSIDE SAMPLE CARD

SLK230

Today's second hand car prices

It is difficult to say whether the face-lifted car is better than the pre-facelift model. In general the face-lifted versions come with slightly better equipment/seats and have an even sturdier body in case of an accident. Naturally they are newer, so they are slightly more expensive.

If two such cars would be offered at the same price, let us say a 1998 model and a 2003 model, the older one tends to be of lower mileage and probably better looked-after. That is why it should be preferable. But at the end it is of course one's personal taste and preference that will make the final decision.

For the author the ideal SLK would be (you have guessed it) the supercharged 230 with manual transmission. An **SLK230** in good condition with full service record, no mechanical or rust issues, can be bought in **the UK** as a pre-facelift model with less than 70k miles on the clock in February 2017 for around £3,800 to 4,400. It seems that these cars, even when properly looked after, do still depreciate, as in summer 2015 similar cars cost around £800 more. And it is surprising that in February 2017 one can still find a few SLK230 in the UK, which have covered less than 50,000 miles. They of course do cost more and start to trade at around £4,700.- to even £7,400 for mint condition vehicles. This is more or less the same value, that such low mileage cars cost back in 2015. In **other parts of Europe** pre-facelift models in similar good condition are more expensive. With around 90,000 km on the clock a SLK230, either manual or auto, will sell for around € 8,800 to 9,300, which is more than in the UK. Prices for similar cars in summer 2015 were some €700 to €900 less, which means they have reached a stage, where people are willing to pay for quality. Cars with less than 50K km on the clock naturally trade at higher levels. They are available between €9,600 €12,500.

This is some €1,000 more than in summer 2015. Pre-facelift cars with around 70,000 miles on the clock cost in **the US** around $7,500 to 8,500, which is more or less the same as in summer 2015. Very few cars are offered, which have traveled less than 50,000 miles.

We have the interesting situation that a good SLK230 with full service history has, as it seems, not bottomed yet in the UK, can hold its value in the US and is on the way up in continental Europe.

For facelift cars in similar conditions with the same mileage add another 10 to 15 percent in all markets. Of course there is and will be always a car that exceeds the evaluation or is much cheaper. So these prices should serve as guideline only. They have been taken from German, French, UK and US car websites over a course of three months from July to Sept. 2015.

Prices in late spring and summer of this year will be slightly higher, as everybody wants a practical convertible. It is difficult to imagine, but the R170 was launched over twenty years ago. That means they are at an age, where the service records and actual condition are more important than its mileage. In the US the automatic version will usually command a slightly higher price of some 5 to 6 percent. In Europe and other parts of the world, prices for manual or automatic cars will be more or less the same. Younger drivers especially in Europe will usually prefer the manual transmission.

Price differences between SLK200 and SLK230 are in most markets minimal at best, given the same age, mileage and condition. This is interesting, as at least in the UK and Continental Europe the SLK 200 is more widely available. In the **US** the **SLK320** trades at around 10 to 15 percent more, when compared to its smaller siblings. In **Europe**, where higher fuel prices and insurance costs can be an issue, this difference in summer 2015 was some five to ten percent only. But now in early 2017, a good condition SLK320 with around 70,000 km on the clock does not sell below €12,500. In the **UK** these cars are hardly available if you look for one that has covered less than 70,000 miles. In early February 2016 only four such cars were offered on car related internet sites. They cost between £4,200 and £6,200. All were offered by traders and carried a three (the cheaper cars) to six months warranty.

The prices quoted before are mostly multi-brand dealer prices. Given the car's age, the SLK R170 is typically no longer offered through the official Daimler-Benz dealer network. If they are at all, they tend to be priced at a premium, partly because of the Mercedes brand dealer's higher overhead and partly because they offer something special that makes it interesting for a Mercedes dealer to take it into his showroom. That can be either low mileage, special edition versions or superior condition. If one is after a certain model in a unique color combination and finds such a car at a Mercedes-Benz dealer, it could be worth the extra money, because those cars have been in almost all cases properly looked after and offer, if you keep such a car for a long while, a potentially good investment.

On top of that, one can in most countries purchase the Daimler-Benz factory two-year warranty for additional assurance. This is the author's experience, at least, through buying second-hand Mercedes cars for the last thirty years. Of course, there will be exceptions to this rule.

The **SLK32 AMG** is a different cup of tea. Priced at $55,500.- when new, with a total sales volume of just 4,333 units, the choices are naturally more limited. The cars are now over ten years old and probably with their third owner. If you are lucky, you can locate an excellent example (and nothing less should be considered) in the **US** with less than 60k miles for some $18,000 to $20,000. With just 263 units exported to the **UK**, it is obvious that the range of choices of SLK32 models are much more limited. Browsing in the UK through the classifieds will usually reveal that no more than just 3 to 4 are for sale at any given time and in most cases, they are silver with the occasional black one in between. Therefore, if you look for a car that is obviously rare, you cannot afford to be too picky regarding color choices.

Go and have a look at the first one that can be found within striking distance. Good ones with complete service records, less than 50,000 miles on the clock, and a full MOT should cost no more than £10,500. That is more or less the same price level being asked for them in 2014. Occasionally one can get examples with double the mileage for less than £6,000.

In Continental **Europe** the SLK32 is nowadays almost equally rare. In Germany for example, the big Internet sites rarely list more than 5 to 6 units for sale at any given time, if you are after a car with less than 100,000 km. All cost in excess of €20,000, and some go even as high as €27,000 with just 40,000 km on the clock. These cars are usually re-imports from Japan. It is the same phenomenon that can be observed (at least in Germany) with late 560SL R107 and SL600 R129, which have all been exported to Japan as lhd cars. It is a habit in Japan to order expensive specialty cars almost always as lhd cars. This should show the neighborhood that you can afford to buy an imported car. “Face” has a lot to do with it.

There is one more thing to say about the AMG versions. It can be assumed that the first and second owner had their priced possession serviced regularly. Even if the values of these cars have increased again lately, its third owner might have bought the car not realizing its costs of maintenance. Although the cars are as dependable as any "standard" SLK, when serviced properly, skimping on maintenance expenses can easily cause major headaches, as AMG-specific parts are very costly.

Therefore, it should be mandatory that an authorized dealer or even indie workshop, which knows the SLK AMG cars, checks the vehicle in question BEFORE your hard-earned money changes hands!

Issues with an AMG SLK can be: bad spark plug wires and ignition coils (they are the cause for misfires) or crankshaft position sensor failures (a warm engine will as a result crank, but start poorly and then run roughly). Depending on what kind of service center one has the car fixed, both repairs can cost between $700 to $1,300 (or the equivalent in euro/pounds sterling).

Another issue can be the intercooler circuit fluid pump, which can (some say: will) fail after around 35,000 mi / 60,000 km. In such a case the supercharger will shut down until air temperature is lower again, then it comes back until air temperature increases one more time, and so forth. That part alone will cost around $800, with labor on top.

A somewhat rare Designo interior will make the car slightly more expensive (if the potential new owner will like it)

If the pump is faulty, it is usually damaged on the inside, which only a mechanic can find out. If the pump looks fine on the inside, you are in luck, because then it is not the pump, but just a blown fuse. It needs to be replaced with a 7.5 amp fuse, a 5 amp fuse will blow again.

I would like to come back one more time to our different points of purchase and see, how prices will vary. Let us stick for this little exercise to the US as country of sale and our SLK230, a face-lifted manual model, from around 2001 with some 60k miles on the clock. That particular car would cost early 2017 at a multi-brand used car dealer somewhere in the US around $12,000. I know that there are differences in what location you plan to buy your car. An official Mercedes dealer at the same location would charge at least around $500 more for the same car. This is a theoretical assumption that an official Mercedes dealer still trades these cars.

If the car has lower mileage and would be of pristine condition, it would cost at a Mercedes dealer not below $14,000. If you wanted to buy that 60k mile car from a private party, the seller would of course try for the dealer price of $12,000 first. He would not find a buyer so easily, if it would have the same condition the car at the multi-brand dealer has to offer. Therefore, the private party will offer the most room of all three for a discount.

But, as many of us have found out the hard way, it would also be the riskiest of all three options. On many occasions we have all experienced in one way or another that the car that was described on the phone, does not turn out to be the car that stands in the seller's driveway. For that reason, the author no longer buys any car from a private party. Most of us have wasted too much time and money looking at cars that did not fit the description.

The prices quoted above are for cars in standard colors and standard equipment. I say that, because rarer "Edition" versions tend to cost a bit more. How much depends on the car's general condition, but a safe bet would be not to pay more than 15 percent on top of the general SLK price. Cars with Designo packages tend to cost around five percent more than the same car without, unless they have one of the more unusual color and that is why rarer combinations. This would justify a surcharge of some 10 percent on the standard SLK's appraised value, if (and that is a big "IF") a prospective owner likes the color and or combination.

For a second or even third hand car, the costs for special equipment are so-called sunken costs, which can usually not be recovered. Some owners of such cars tend to disagree, but one will have a very hard time recovering $3,500 or even a suitable fraction of it for a Designo package that has graced a car that is already over 10 years old.

By the way, there is a fourth possibility to buy cars and that is at auctions. Occasionally you can get great deals from them, but at the same time you can also get carried away by audience frenzy and end up paying way too much for a car. The author stays away from auctions, as the cars sold there can in most instances not be properly assessed.

Manual cars are usually cheaper in the US, but are preferred by younger drivers in Europe and the UK

List of differences between the R170 model years

Most of these differences have been mentioned already in the previous chapters, but it might be beneficial for the reader, to have them all included in a separate chapter for easier reference. These upgrades usually happened towards the mid of the year. In the US and some other export markets these cars were then sold as next year's models.

Changes for 1997 on cars built after August 1, 1997:

- A black fixed-mast antenna, installed on the left rear quarter-panel replaced the antenna hidden in the bumper. People had noted that it offered in some locations poor radio reception. Some cars built before this date had the antenna retrofitted at the request of the owner
- Brake Assist System BAS was part of the standard equipment
- Exterior color Polar White was changed in some markets to Glacier White.

Changes for 1998 on cars built after June 1, 1998:

- Telephone Package K1: Integrated mobile cellular telephone and CD changer option was dropped
- Telephone Package K2: Integrated portable cellular telephone and CD changer option was introduced: they were slightly different and had the new fiber optic connection. The new CD changer won't work with the older cars
- A new audio system with cassette player with fiber optic link to the CD changer was introduced. It offered integrated controls for a cellular phone
- The left side of the passenger foot-well received a net for additional storage
- The interior was equipped with an auto-dimmer feature
- In the US the five-speed manual transmission became available
- AMG Sports Package (SP 1) was added as option
- Anti tow-away feature was added

For some markets, various color options were either dropped, added or moved to the options/special orders list in 1998:

- Obsidian Black metallic and Calypso Green paints were moved to the special-order list
- Black Opal metallic paint was dropped
- Magma Red paint was added and replaced Imperial Red paint
- Firemist Red paint was added
- Navy-Charcoal interior color option was moved to the special-order list

Changes after October 19th, 1998:

- Cruise Control was added standard to all cars with manual transmission.
- Scheduled maintenance was now included for the US in the purchase price
- Designo line was introduced with two packages: Designo Electric Green (green metallic paint with an interior finished in charcoal leather and trim with light green) and Designo Copper (copper metallic paint with an interior finished with copper and two-tone charcoal leather).

Changes for 1999 on cars built after June 1, 1999:

- Telephone Package K2 with CD changer: Integrated portable cellular phone operated digitally instead of previously analog with new Motorola Startac phone. It can be retrofitted into earlier 1999 SLK models
- Telephone Package 2a with CD-changer offered Voice-activated digital portable phone

Changes for 2000 on all SLKs built after February 1, 2000:

Exterior:

- Restyled front and rear bumpers with body-colored apron
- Side skirts and door handles in body color
- Polished stainless steel exhaust tip
- Turn-signals were moved from the side of the front fenders into the exterior mirrors

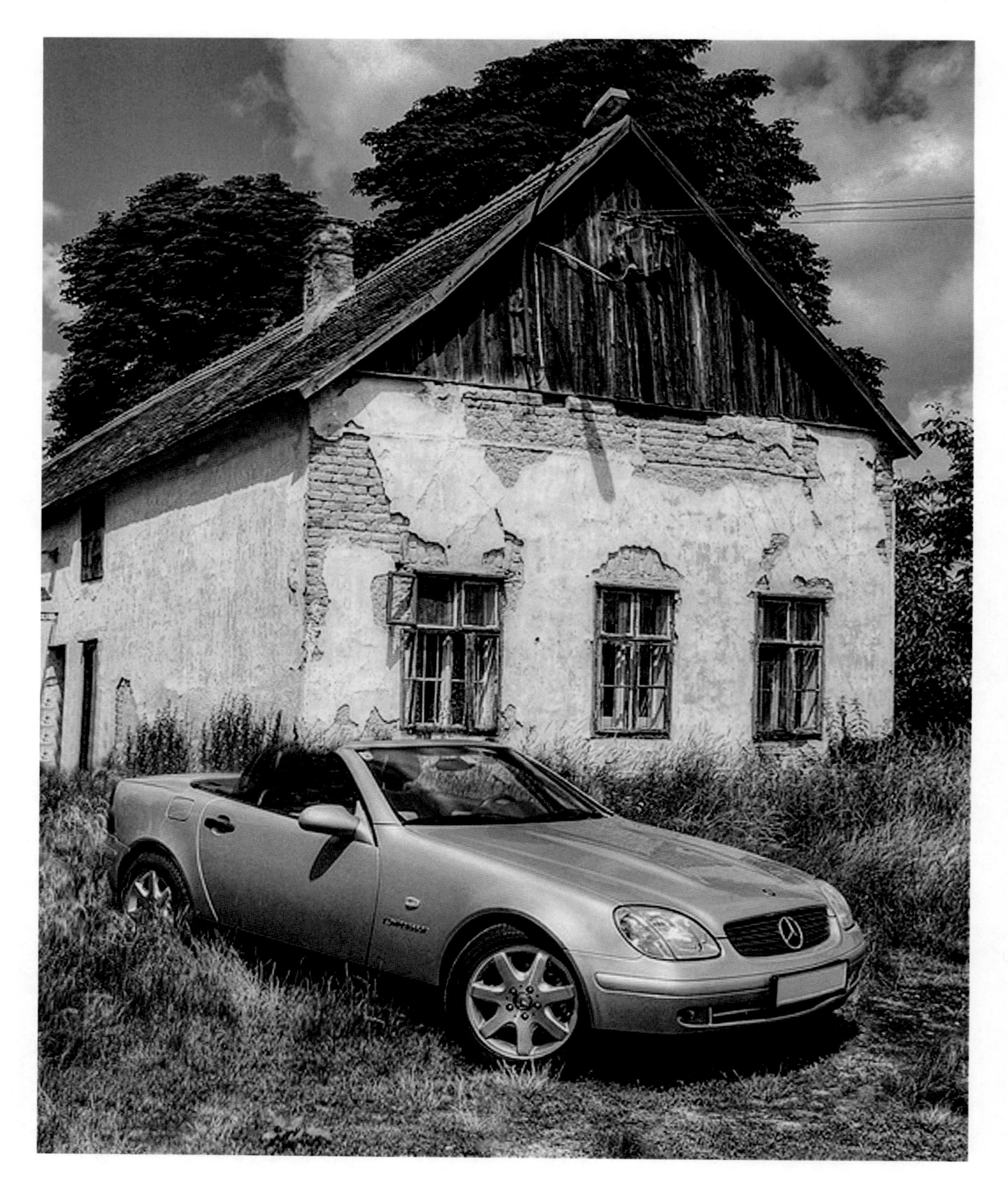

- Trunk latch release was moved from right side of the trunk to the center of the trunk above the license plate
- Tail light lenses were slightly re-styled
- Calypso Green paint was discontinued
- Sapphire Blue paint became a special order color

Interior:

- The manually adjustable telescoping steering wheel was no longer standard equipment as it was in 1996 – 1999 models
- Redesigned seats with better support
- Redesigned steering wheel in two-tone color to match interior
- Redesigned gear shift knob (automatic and manual)
- Machined aluminum interior trim replaced simulated carbon fiber trim
- New door sill panels with "SLK" logo
- New interior light with integrated telephone microphone, garage door opener, and interior intrusion sensor
- Chrome button on handbrake
- New interior colors: Crimson Red - Charcoal Citrus, Sienna Beige – Charcoal
- Available as special order: Yellow – Charcoal and Marlin Blue - Charcoal
- Other optional interior colors: Oyster - Charcoal, Navy Blue - Charcoal, Salsa Red – Charcoal
- Eight-way adjustable power seats and manually adjustable telescoping steering wheel was optional.

Other Equipment:

- Fuel tank capacity increased from 53 l (12 gallons) to 60 l (14 gallons)
- Strengthened uni-body and thicker sheet-metal of the ellipsoid firewall
- Revised front stabilizer bar, new rear stabilizer bar
- A 3.46:1 axle ratio, optional for the manual shift SLK, was dropped in the US
- Electronic Stability Program ESP was added
- Six-speed manual transmission replaced five-speed version
- TouchShift became standard with automatic transmissions
- Steering box was repositioned due to longer 3.2 l power plant
- Tele-Aid emergency call system was added
- Gear selector display near odometer for automatic transmissions
- Maintenance indicator, integrated into the digital display field for the odometer, was enlarged for better visibility
- K4 Package-Xenon headlamps with heated headlamp washers and dynamic head light adjuster became available as option

- AMG SP1 Package included silver-painted radiator and intercooler grills
- K2 and K2a packages were not available on early production face-lifted SLKs

Equipment specific to SLK230:

- New six-spoke alloys, 7.0J x 16 front, 8.0J x 16 rear
- Power output increased to 197 hp at 5,500 rpm (previously 193 at 5,300 rpm).

Equipment specific to SLK320:

- Unique front apron
- Eucalyptus wood with a combination leather/wood steering wheel was standard with Solid Charcoal and Sienna - Charcoal interiors
- Darkened birds-eye maple wood with a combination leather/wood steering wheel was standard with Crimson - Charcoal, Citrus - Charcoal and Marlin - Charcoal interiors
- Eight-way adjustable power seats and manually adjustable telescoping steering wheel were standard
- New door sill panels with "V6" logo
- Larger brakes
- Unique five-spoke alloys, 7.0J x 16 front, 8.0J x 16 rear.

A bespoke interior by "Vilner"

Unique SLKs

BMW was about to launch its Z3 Coupe and Daimler-Benz management tinkered at the end of the 1990s with the idea to offer the SLK in closed form as well. Various designs had been proposed with the rear coming from either the A-class, C-class or even M-class.

Although there is hardly any information available, it is believed that the car should come as two-seater with sufficient storage capacity for an extended vacation. It should be offered with all engines that were available for the standard SLK. Once BMW had introduced its M Coupe, AMG should come with its own alternative. At the end those plans were dropped in favor of the C-class Sportcoupe, which became available in 2000.

This and the next four photos are sourced from relatively small originals, hence the unfortunately not optimal quality.

This was a more elegant (or less hideous) looking study with a large rear window

The following photos are in no particular order and should only demonstrate the car's attractiveness for further body tuning

Lambo-style doors and a cautious attempt to copy the R171 front by Rieger Tuning

This Belgian conversion with an R171 front looks more convincing

An attempt to bring back some of the Koenig Special body kits

Also the interior was heavily modified

This appears to be a private conversion

Now…is it or is it not?

As you can see, it still is the R170, this time in a more successful attempt by Rieger to disguise its origins

And in case you also wanted the rear to look like an SL R230, Rieger did that too

Another interesting project was an SLK that was based on the sturdy all-terrain G-class. Jim Rogers, a former US hedge-fund manager took his sunburst-yellow SLK look-a-like from 1999 till 2001 on a 100,000 mile tour around the world in order, as he mentioned, to document the state of the world at the end of the millenium. Naturally he did not create his car himself, this terrific job was initiated by Harald Pietschmann, an engineer, automotive designer and 4x4 consultant. Pietschmann had been involved with 4x4 conversions for quite some time and even dreamed of combining the chassis of a G-class with the body of a R107 SL for himself, as both cars have the same wheelbase. When Rogers asked him to conceptualize a 4x4 diesel car with convertible body, he had a Porsche on a Toyota S70 chassis in mind. But Pietschmann convinced him to choose two Mercedes instead. As the new SLK had the same wheelbase as the old SL and G-class, this car was preferred over the SL due to its more durable vario-roof. The project was designed by Gerhard Steinle, former head of Daimler-Benz Advanced Design and executed by Metalcrafters, a company that specializes in show cars and prototypes. In order to have sufficient storage a trailer was built that is a copy of the SLK's trunk.

1 G + 1 SLK = 1 4x4 GLK

Rogers started with his future wife Page Parker in the car that he called Mercedes GLK ("G" from G-class and "LK" from SLK) on January 1st 1999 in Iceland. When the tour was completed, it was January 5th 2002, 1101 days later. The couple had crossed six continents, explored 116 countries and had planned to drive some 150,000 km. At the end, it was slightly more: 245,000 km. What an adventure!

Somewhere in Mongolia (all GLK photos are courtesy of Jim Rogers)

Crossing the Pakistan-Indian border

Freshly cleaned, car and trailer get loaded onto a wooden trawler for an ocean crossing into Oman

Jim Rogers in front of an Indonesian pagoda

Technical specifications

GENERAL DATA:

Years of Manufacture: July 1996 – April 2004

Price at Introduction:

SLK200:	52,900.- DM (1996)
SLK200 K:	55,950.- DM (1996), only Southern Europe
SLK230 K:	60,950.- DM (1996)
SLK200 K:	30,000.- € (2000)
SLK230 K:	33,000.- € (2000)
SLK320:	38,800.- € (2000)
SLK32 AMG:	56,000.- € (2001)

Chassis/Body: Steel Unit Body

Exterior Dimensions:

Total Length:	157.5 inches (4,050 mm)
Total Width:	67.7 inches (1,720 mm)
Height at curb weight:	50.4 inches (1,281 mm)
Wheelbase:	94.5 inches (2,400 mm)

Curb Weight:

SLK200:	2,579 lb (1,170 kg)
SLK200 K:	2,728 lb (1,240 kg)
SLK230 K:	2,701 lb (1,225 kg)
SLK 200K:	2,789 lb (1,265 kg)
SLK230 K:	2,833 lb (1,285 kg)
SLK320:	2,877 lb (1,305 kg)
SLK32 AMG:	3,075 lb (1,395 kg)

Fuel Tank:	
All models:	15.8 gal. (60 liters), pre-facelift: 13.9 gal (53 l)
Turning Circle:	34.7 ft (10.58 m), AMG: 34.5 ft (10.52 m)
	The better result for the SLK32 is due to its tires
Drag Coefficient:	0.35 (SLK200)

ENGINES:

SLK200 (1996), 170.435:	4 Cylinder M111 E20, 111.946 L4
Capacity:	121.9 cu inches (1,999 cc)
Configuration:	Front mounted, longitudinal, inline
Head:	Pushrod and rocker actuated ohv, DOHC, 16 valv.
Fuel System:	VDO MSE (1996-98), ME (1998-00)
Bore and Stroke:	3.50 x 3.07 inches (89.9 x 78.7 mm)
Aspiration:	Natural
Power:	136 DIN hp @ 5.500 rpm
Torque:	190 Nm @ 3.700 rpm (140 ft/lb)
Compression Ratio:	1:10.4

SLK200 K (1996), 170.444:	4 Cylinder M111 E20 ML, 111.943 L4
Capacity:	121.9 cu inches (1,999 cc)
Configuration:	Front mounted, longitudinal, inline
Head:	Pushrod and rocker actuated ohv, DOHC, 16 valv
Fuel System:	Bosch ME 2.1 Motronic
Bore and Stroke:	3.50 x 3.07 inches (89.9 x 78.7 mm)
Aspiration:	Roots Kompressor, Eaton-type
Power:	192 DIN hp @ 5.300 rpm
Torque:	270 Nm @ 2.700 rpm (199.1 ft/lb)
Compression Ratio:	1:8.5

SLK230 K (1996), 170.447:	4 Cylinder M111 E23 ML, 111.973 L4
Capacity:	140.0 cu inches (2,295 cc)
Configuration:	Front mounted, longitudinal, inline
Head:	Pushrod and rocker actuated ohv, DOHC, 16 valv
Fuel System:	Bosch ME 2.1 Motronic
Bore and Stroke:	3.54 x 3.46 inches (90.9 x 88.4 mm)
Aspiration:	Roots Kompressor, Eaton type
Power:	193 DIN hp @ 5.300 rpm
Torque:	280 Nm @ 2.500 rpm (206.5 ft/lb)
Compression Ratio:	1:8.8

SLK200 K (2000), 170.445:	4 Cylinder M111 E20 ML, 111.985 L4
Capacity:	121.9 cu inches (1,999 cc)
Configuration:	Front mounted, longitudinal, inline
Head:	Pushrod and rocker actuated ohv, ohc, 16 valves
Fuel System:	Bosch ME 2.1 Motronic
Bore and Stroke:	3.50 x 3.07 inches (89.9 x 78.7 mm)
Aspiration:	Roots Kompressor, Eaton type
Power:	163 DIN hp @ 5.300 rpm
Torque:	230 Nm @ 2.500 rpm (170 ft/lb)
Compression Ratio:	1:9.5

SLK230 K (2000), 170.449:	4 Cylinder M111 E23 ML, 111.983 L4
Capacity:	140.0 cu inches (2,295 cc)
Configuration:	Front mounted, longitudinal, inline
Head:	Pushrod and rocker actuated ohv, ohc, 16 valves
Fuel System:	Bosch ME 2.1 Motronic
Bore and Stroke:	3.54 x 3.46 inches (90.9 x 88.4 mm)
Aspiration:	Roots Kompressor, Eaton type
Power:	197 DIN hp @ 5.500 rpm
Torque:	280 Nm @ 2.500 rpm (206.5 ft/lb)
Compression Ratio:	1:9.0

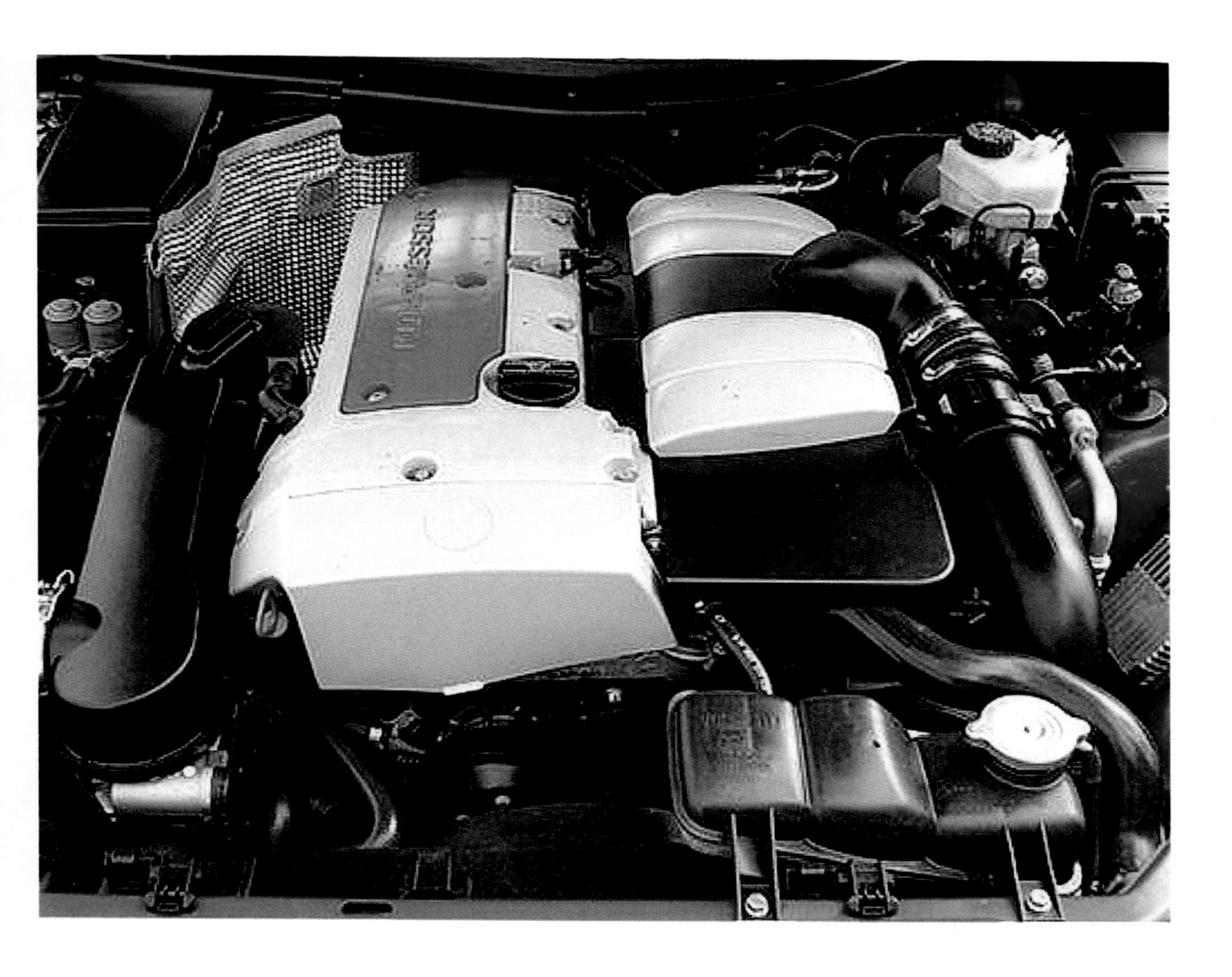

SLK320 (2000), 170.465:	6 Cylinder M112 E32, 112.947 V6
Capacity:	195.2 cu inches (3,199 cc)
Configuration:	Front mounted, longitudinal, inline
Head:	Pushrod and rocker actuated ohv,SOHC, 18 valves
Fuel System:	Bosch ME 2.8 Motronic
Bore and Stroke:	3.54 x 3.31 inches (89.9 x 84.0 mm)
Aspiration:	Natural
Power:	218 DIN hp @ 5.700 rpm
Torque:	310 Nm @ 3.000 rpm (228 ft/lb)
Compression Ratio:	1:9.0

SLK32 AMG (2000), 170.466:	6 Cylinder M112 E32 ML, 112.960 V6
Capacity:	195.2 cu inches (3,199 cc)
Configuration:	Front mounted, longitudinal, inline
Head:	Pushrod and rocker actuated ohv,SOHC, 18 valves
Fuel System:	Bosch MPFI
Bore and Stroke:	3.54 x 3.31 inches (89.9 x 84.0 mm)
Aspiration:	Lysholm Kompressor
Power:	354 DIN hp @ 6.100 rpm
Torque:	450 Nm @ 2.500 rpm (332 ft/lb)
Compression Ratio:	1:9.0

PERFORMANCE:

0-62 mph (0-100 km/h):

SLK200 (1996):	9.7 seconds
SLK200 K (1996):	7.6 seconds
SLK230 K (1996):	7.6 seconds
SLK 200K (2000):	8.2 seconds
SLK230 K (2000):	7.2 seconds
SLK320 (2000):	6.9 seconds
SLK32 AMG (2001):	5.2 seconds

Maximum speed:

SLK200 (1996):	208 km/h (129 mph)
SLK200 K (1996):	231 km/h (143 mph)
SLK230 K (1996):	231 km/h (143 mph)
SLK 200K (2000):	223 km/h (138 mph)
SLK230 K (2000):	240 km/h (149 mph)
SLK320 (2000):	245 km/h (152 mph)
SLK32 AMG (2001):	250 km/h (155 mph) electronically limited

Fuel consumption:

SLK200 (1996):	9.1 l/100km (25 mpg)
SLK200 K (1996):	9.3 l/100km (25 mpg)
SLK230 K (1996):	9.3 l/100km (25 mpg)
SLK 200K (2000):	9 6 l/100km (24 mpg)
SLK230 K (2000):	9.8 l/100km (24 mpg)
SLK320 (2000):	11.1 l/100km (21 mpg)
SLK32 AMG (2001):	11.2 l/100km (21 mpg)

DRAG TIMES:

0 – ¼ mile:

SLK200 (1996):	19.6 seconds
SLK200 K (1996):	14.9 seconds
SLK230 K (1996):	14.8 seconds
SLK 200K (2000):	15.7 seconds
SLK230 K (2000):	14.7 seconds
SLK320 (2000):	14.3 seconds
SLK32 AMG (2001):	13.1 seconds

Speed at ¼ mile:

SLK200 (1996):	135 km/h (84 mph)
SLK200 K (1996):	149 km/h (93 mph)
SLK230 K (1996):	150 km/h (93 mph)
SLK 200K (2000):	142 km/h (88 mph)
SLK230 K (2000):	150 km/h (93 mph)
SLK320 (2000):	156 km/h (97 mph)
SLK32 AMG (2001):	174 km/h (108 mph)

0 – 1km:

SLK200 (1996):	30.2 seconds
SLK200 K (1996):	27.3 seconds
SLK230 K (1996):	27.1 seconds
SLK 200K (2000):	28.8 seconds
SLK230 K (2000):	27.0 seconds
SLK320 (2000):	26.2 seconds
SLK32 AMG (2001):	23.8 seconds

Power to weight ratio:

SLK200 (1996):	83.7 watt/kg (38.0 watt/lb)
SLK200 K (1996):	112.8 watt/kg (51.2 watt/lb)
SLK230 K (1996):	113.6 watt/kg (51.1 watt/lb)
SLK 200K (2000):	93.0 watt/kg (42.2 watt/lb)
SLK230 K (2000):	110.7 watt/kg (50.2 watt/lb)
SLK320 (2000):	120.3 watt/kg (54.6 watt/lb)
SLK32 AMG (2001):	183.1 watt/kg (83.1 watt/lb)

Weight to power ratio:

SLK200 (1996):	12.0 kg/kW (8.8 kg/hp, 19.7 lbs/hp)
SLK200 K (1996):	8.9 kg/kW (6.5 kg/hp, 14.6 lbs/hp)
SLK230 K (1996):	8.8 kg/kW (6.5 kg/hp, 14.5 lbs/hp)
SLK 200K (2000):	10.8 kg/kW (7.9 kg/hp, 17.7 lbs/hp)
SLK230 K (2000):	9.0 kg/kW (6.6 kg/hp, 14.9 lbs/hp)
SLK320 (2000):	8.3 kg/kW (6.1 kg/hp, 13.6 lbs/hp)
SLK32 AMG (2001):	5.5 kg/kW (4.0 kg/hp, 9.0 lbs/hp)

Co2 emissions:

SLK200 (1996):	217 g/km
SLK200 K (1996):	220 g/km
SLK230 K (1996):	220 g/km
SLK 200K (2000):	231 g/km
SLK230 K (2000):	236 g/km
SLK320 (2000):	267 g/km
SLK32 AMG (2001):	261 g/km

TRANSMISSION:

6-speed Manual:	1st: 4.46:1
	2nd: 2.61:1
	3rd: 1.72:1
	4th: 1.24:1
	5th: 1:1
	6th: 0:84
5-speed Automatic:	1st: 3.93:1 (SLK32 AMG: 3.59)
	2nd: 2.41:1 (SLK32 AMG: 2.19)
	3rd: 1.49:1 (SLK32 AMG:1.41)
	4th: 1.00:1
	5th: 0.83:1

Clutch:	Single cushion disc, dry plate clutch (man.trans.)

Rear axle ratio:	
SLK200 (1996):	3.29 (5-speed automatic: 3.91)
SLK200 K (1996):	3.46
SLK230 K (1996):	3.46 (5-speed automatic: 3.27)
SLK200 K (2000):	3.46 (5-speed automatic: 3.27)
SLK230 K (2000):	3.46 (5-speed automatic: 3.27)
SLK320 (2000):	3.27
SLK32 AMG (2001):	3.06

CHASSIS:	
Exhaust:	Single tail-pipe
Suspension:	
Front:	Independent McPherson, coil springs, anti-roll bar
Rear:	Multilink, coil springs, anti-roll bar
Steering:	Recirculating ball, 3 turns
Brakes:	
Front:	Vented disc 288 mm (11.3 in)
Rear:	Vented disc 278 mm (11 in)
Brakes SLK32:	
Front:	Vented disc 334 mm (13.2 in)
Rear:	Vented disc 300 mm (11.8 in)
Tires SLK200:	205/60 R15 V (front and rear), also 200K 2000
Tires SLK230 K, 320:	205/55 R16 V (F), 225/50 R16 V (R)
	(also 200K 1996)
Tires AMG standard:	225/45 ZR17 (F), 245/40 ZR17 (R),
	other sizes optional

V6

Power and torque curves

SLK200, 1996: 136 HP at 5,500 rpm, 190 NM (140 ft-lbs) at 3,700 rpm

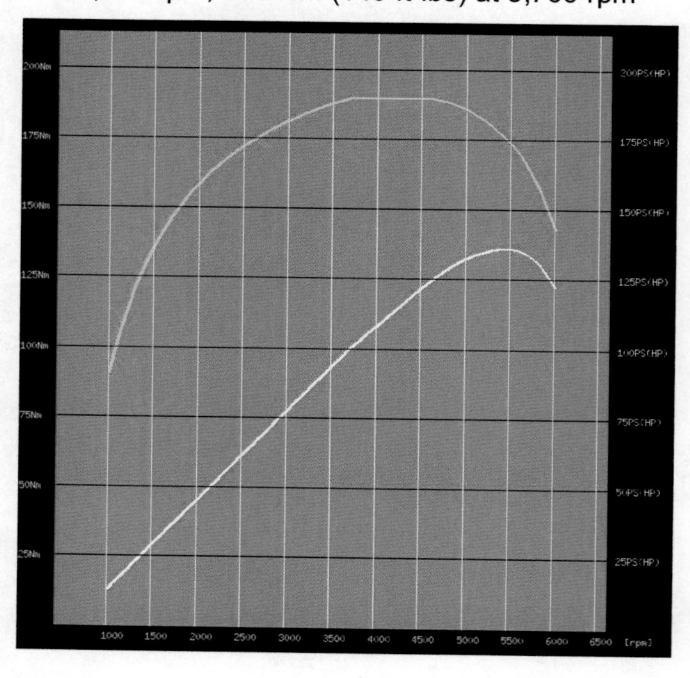

SLK200 K, 1996: 192 HP at 5,300 rpm, 270 NM (199 ft-lbs) at 2,700 rpm

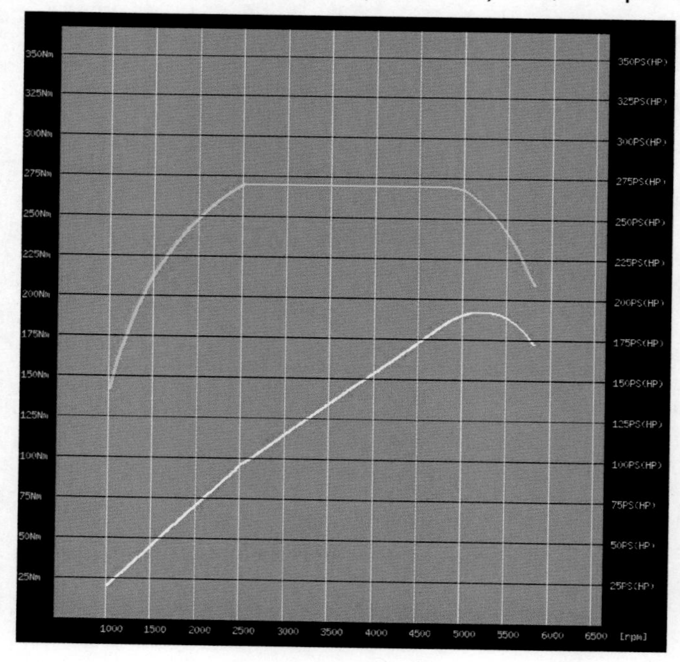

SLK230 K, 1996: 193 HP at 5,300 rpm, 280 NM (207 ft-lbs) at 2,500 rpm

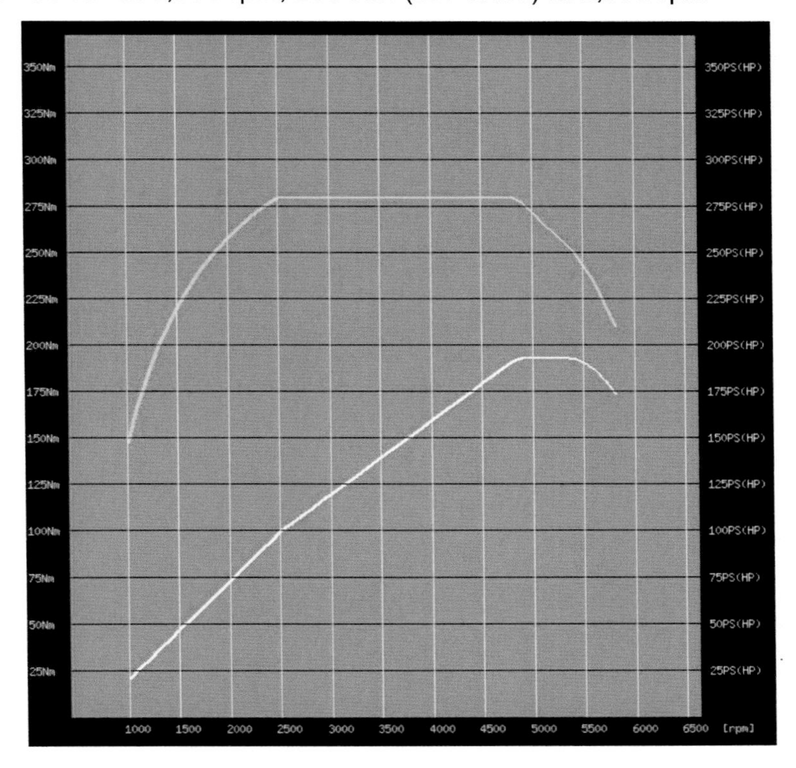

SLK200 K, 2000: 163 HP at 5,300 rpm, 230 NM (170 ft-lbs) at 2,500 rpm

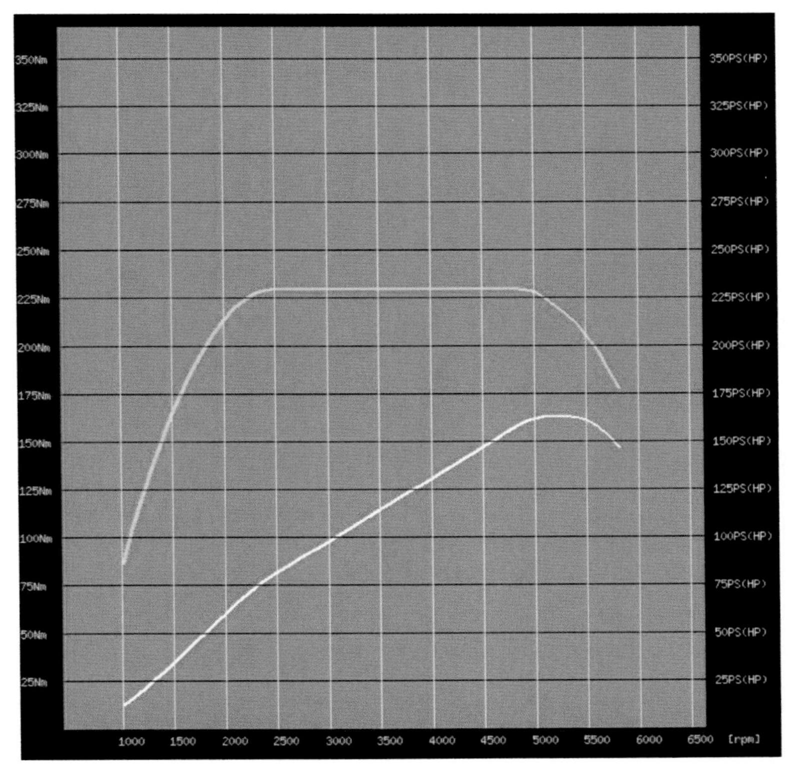

SLK230 K, 2000: 197 HP at 5,500 rpm, 280 NM (206 ft-lbs) at 2,500 rpm

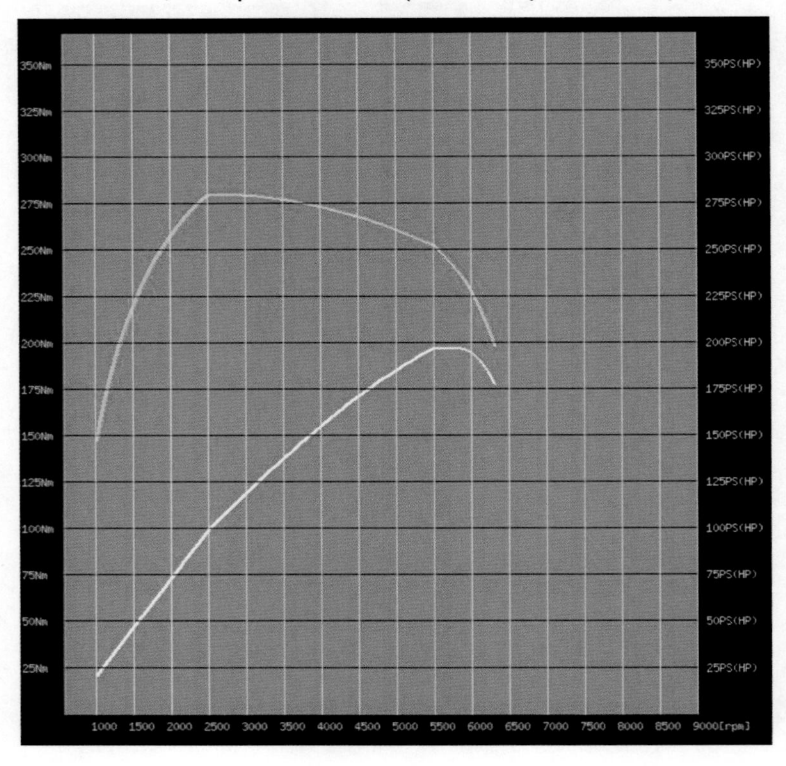

SLK320, 2000: 218 HP at 5,700 rpm, 310 NM (229 ft-lbs) at 3,000 rpm

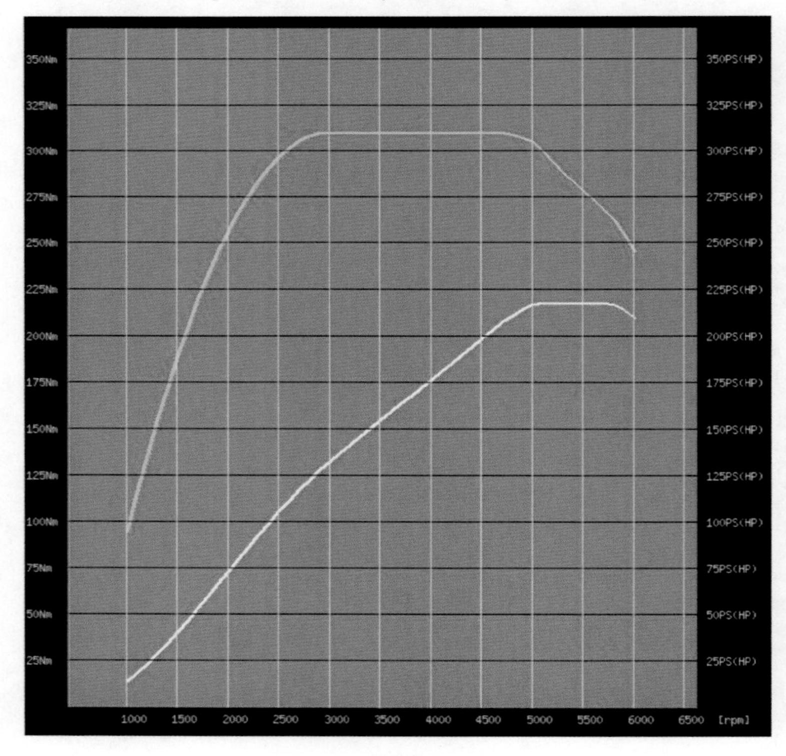

SLK32 AMG, 2001: 354 HP at 6,100 rpm, 450 NM (332 ft-lbs) at 2,500 rpm

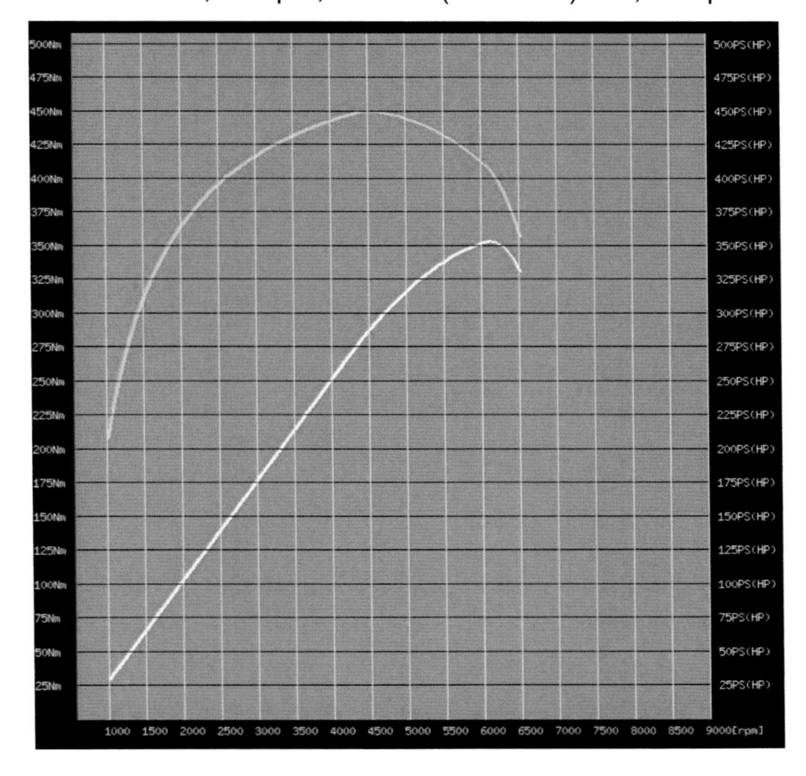

Production data

Type	Code	1995	1996	1997	1998	1999	2000	Total
SLK200	170435	12	2.798	12.104	13.187	15.925	820	**44.846**
SLK200K	170444	1	358	3.651	4.607	3.431	305	**12.353**
SLK230K	170447	18	5.023	32.390	37.028	36.789	2.272	**113.520**
Total		**31**	**8.179**	**48.145**	**54.822**	**56.145**	**3.397**	**170.719**

Type	Code	1999	2000	2001	2002	2003	2004	Total	Grand Total
SLK200K	170445	26	15.898	16.550	11.581	9.811	1.583	**55.449**	**100.295**
SLK230K	170449	77	15.860	13.152	9.987	7.260	969	**47.305**	**59.658**
SLK320	170465	67	14.002	10.287	5.340	3.377	343	**33.416**	**146.936**
SLK32	170466		10	2.193	1.336	742	52	**4.333**	**8.666**
Total		**170**	**45.770**	**42.182**	**28.244**	**21.190**	**2.947**	**140.503**	**311.222**

A torrential rainfall is one way to check, whether the roof is leaking ☺

Acknowledgements

This book would not have been possible without the invaluable information from the Daimler AG archives and from websites such as SLKworld.com and benzworld.org.

Other principal sources for the book in alphabetical order:

Autobild Okt. 1996, Jan. 1999, Sept. 2003; autobild.de/klassik 20.04.2008, 30.01.2019; automotive.com, automuseum-stuttgart.de; classicdriver.com; auto motor und sport Aug. 1994, Jan. 1996, März 1996, Feb. 1998, April 1999, März 2000, Aug. 2001, April 2003, emercedesbenz.com, germancarforum.com, "Mercedes-Benz Automobile, Band 2,

1964 – Heute", H. Hofner, H. Schrader; Motor Klassik Jan. 2011

Own archives

All design-, production-, technical- or test-photos and drawings are courtesy of the Daimler AG archives,

Some photos of the SLK are provided by Daimler AG, tuned car photos are by the respective tuning companies.

Photos of the Brabus SLK on pages 111 – 117 are by M. Normann

Photos of the Jim Rogers GLK on pages 174 - 177 are by Jim Rogers

Other photos are by Bernd S. Koehling or from his collection

SLK 230

Other books by the author

Printed books:

MB, The 170 series: from the 1936 170V to the 170S Cabriolet

MB, The 1950s Volume 1: from the 170V to the 300Sc Roadster

MB, The 1950s Volume 2: from the 180 Ponton to the 300SL Roadster

MB, The 1950s, The 300 Series: from the 300 Sedan to the 300Sc Cabriolet

MB, The 1950s, The Ponton Series: from the 180 Sedan to the 220SE Cabriolet

MB, The 1960s Volume 1: from the 190c to the 280SE 3.5 Cabriolet

MB, The 1960s Volume 2: from the 230SL and 600 to the 300SEL 6.3

MB, The 1960s, W111/112C: from the 220 Coupe to the 280SE 3.5 Cabriolet

MB, The 1960s, W112: from the 300SE to the 300SE Cabriolet

MB, The 1960s, W108/109 six-cylinder Sedan

MB, The 1960s, W108/109 V8 Sedan

MB, The 1970s: W116: From the 280S to the 450SEL 6.9 Sedan

MB, The early SL cars: from the 300SL Gullwing to the 280SL Pagoda *

MB, The modern SL: The R107 from 1971 – 1989

MB, The modern SL, The R129 from 1989 – 2001

MB, The modern SL: The R230 from 2001 – 2011

MB, The SLK R170 from 1996 – 2004

MB, The SLK R171 from 2004 – 2011

MB, The SLK R172 from 2011 onwards

**The early SL cars are also part of the two books: 1950s and 1960s, Volume 2*

E-books:

MB, The 170V and 170S (W136) Sedan, OTP and Cabriolets from 1936 – 1955

MB, The 1950s: The 220 (W187) Sedan, Cabriolets and OTP from 1951 – 1955

MB, The 1950s: The 300 (W186, W189, 1951 – 1962) and 300S, Sc (W188, 1951 – 1958)

MB, The 1950s: The 180, 190 (W120, W121) Ponton Sedan from 1953 – 1962

MB, The 1950s: The 219, 220a, S, SE (W 105, W180, W128) Ponton from 1954 – 1960

MB, The 1950s: The 190SL (W121) from 1955 – 1963 and Max Hoffman

MB, The 1950s: The 300SL (W198) Coupe and Roadster from 1954 – 1963

MB, The 1960s: The 220b, 230S (W111) Sedan from 1959 – 1968

MB, The 1960s: The 190c, 200, 230 (W110) Sedan from 1961 – 1968

MB, The 1960s: The 220, 250, 280, 300SE (W111, W112) Cpe/Cabrio from 1961 – 1971

MB, The 1960s: The 300SE, 300SEC (W112), 1961 – 1967

MB, The 1960s: The 230, 250, 280SL (W113) Pagoda from 1963 – 1971

MB, The 1960s: The 600 (W100), 1963 – 1981

MB, The 1960s: The 250, 280, 300 (W108, W109) six-cylinder Sedan from 1965 – 1972

MB, The 1960s: The 280, 300 (W108, W109) V8 Sedan from 1967 – 1972

MB, The 1970s: The 280, 300, 350, 450, 6.9 (W116) Sedan from 1972 – 1980

MB, The SLK R170 from 1996 – 2004

MB, The SLK R171 from 2004 – 2011

MB, The SLK R172 from 2011 onwards

MB, The modern SL: The R107 from 1971 – 1989

MB, The modern SL: The R129 from 1989 – 2001

MB, The modern SL: The R230 from 2001 – 2011

MB, The modern SL: The R231 from 2012 onwards

There is one more thing

You have now reached the last page of this book and I sincerely hope that you have liked reading about the history of the first SLK models. I also hope that you have liked the photos and that you have found information about these cars that you have not found otherwise. Should you have bought the book through Amazon, you have the opportunity to rate it. Your comments will then appear in the review list of my books. If you believe this book is worth sharing, would you be so kind and take a few seconds to let other Mercedes enthusiasts know about it. Maybe they would be grateful. As a small volume author, I will be for sure, as it will help me to gain a bit of recognition. If you will find the time to write a short review, I would like to offer you a **small gift**. You can choose one of my 23 Mercedes e-books and I will send it to your e-mail address free. Of course, I will never spam you.

Please let me know via e-mail, where you have written your review. Here is my e-mail address: bernd@benz-books.com

This book has been printed by an Amazon affiliate printing house, which means that I have unfortunately no control over its printing quality. Should you have received a copy that does not meet your expectations from a printing point of view, please do both of us a favor and ask Amazon for a replacement. Thank you very much for your kind understanding,

Alles Gute,
Bernd

Made in the USA
Las Vegas, NV
21 August 2023